EXTREME ROMANCE

A Single's Guide to Building True Love

Jesse and Heidi Jost

ISBN: 978-0-9864963-0-1

Published by Josephine Publishing
P.O. Box 314
Milk River, Alberta T0K 1M0
www.josephinepublishing.com

Cover design: Josiah Jost, www.siahdesign.com
Cover photos: iStockphoto, www.istockphoto.com
Photographer: iofoto, www.iofoto.com
Interior design: Jesse Jost and Josiah Jost

To contact Jesse and Heidi or order books
see page 159

Printed in the United States by Morris Publishing®
3212 East Highway 30
Kearney, NE 68847
1-800-650-7888

TABLE OF CONTENTS

ACKNOWLEDGEMENTS

I am so grateful to God for inventing the amazing gifts of romance, love, and physical intimacy, and the safe place of marriage to enjoy them. If it weren't for God's goodness, creativity, and abundant extravagance, we would have nothing to write about.

I am more thankful than this keyboard can express for my amazing co-author and wife Heidi. She makes me thrilled to wake up each morning and life becomes a wondrous delight the moment she walks in the room. I love being with you, Sweetheart. If I said even half the things that I appreciate about you, I would lose all our readers before they even got to chapter one, so I'll save the rest of my thanks to you for later.

I also want to thank my parents and Heidi's parents for the gifts of purity and protection that they gave us. They were so diligent to raise us for God's glory and instill in us a love for our great Creator and to always point us to Him. Many of the truths this book contains were taught to us at an early age and for this we are deeply thankful. We are reaping untold rewards for their sacrifice. I pray that we can do the same for our John-Michael and Sophia.

We sent the first drafts of this book to many of our friends. Each one who read it had some very helpful advice and perspectives which really helped clarify what we meant and what we didn't mean. Because of them you hopefully will find less to trip over and more to chew on. Among those read our drafts were: Erin Langemann, Rebecca Fehr, Timothy Lipp, Josiah Jost, Emily Jost, Lisa Jost, Megan Kenyon, Reid Wilkie, Arlo Schulz, Lydia Collin, Leandra Phillips, Betsy Schultz, Moriah Kembel, Amanda Piechnik, Jacob Denhollander and Alisha Roby. I also want to thank Loraine Wahl (Heidi's mom) and my brother Jonathan for taking time out of their busy schedules to proofread the final copy.

So much prayer has gone into this book; I continue to pray that it will be used by God to reveal more of His character and will revolutionize your life in the area of romantic love and physical intimacy. I want God to be glorified in spite of my fumbling attempts to share His breathtaking goodness. Please contact us if you take issue with anything in this book (**Heidi:** or even if you don't!). Heidi and I are both eager to learn and want to be teachable about any belief that we might hold in error.

God is the giver of all good gifts. I pray that in the following pages you will be inspired to want more of Him and to gain a deeper longing for the extreme romance and pleasure that He alone can provide.

Jesse Jost, November, 2009

INTRODUCTION

Brad Paisley muses in a song that "if love was a plane, nobody'd get on." Why? Because, he sings, "there's a six in ten chance [the plane would be] going down." The odds of having a successful, vibrant, lifelong relationship are less than forty percent. Almost half of marriages end in divorce, and who knows what percentage of the couples who do stay together are doing it for love, not just for financial or pragmatic reasons?

Thankfully, contrary to the popular view, love is not like the lottery. You don't have to nibble your nails hoping that you'll get lucky and fall into lifelong love. Love is a choice and a good marriage is something you work toward. It's a lot like music. If you hope to pick up the perfect instrument and instantly make beautiful music with it, well, sorry to break it to you – but it's not going to happen. If you want to play an instrument well it will take a lot of time and commitment. Years of practice are required to play some instruments really well. So it is with marriage. Achieving a good marriage takes work and discipline. I know this runs contrary to the romance novels and chick flick movies that depict true love as a by-product of the right chemical combination. People who buy into that philosophy need to get out of the lab and into the real world.

Infatuation and hormones can trick you into thinking that fairytale, work-free love exists, but that kind of imaginary love won't last. Millions of broken hearts testify to this reality. But you don't have to become a cynic about love and marriage; you need to become a realist, because real true romance does exist and it is more satisfying than you can imagine. I know. I taste it regularly.

True love takes work. Keeping yourself pure and marrying the first person you give your heart to won't automatically create true love. Asking the father first and "doing courtship" won't guarantee it either. This book is not promising that proper procedure or keeping yourself pure will guarantee a perfect marriage. As someone who has been married for almost four years, I've seen firsthand how the initial rush of feelings wears off and the newness and excitement peters out. The wonderful love story that was running on automatic during the thrills of new love now switches to manual gear and we find it's ultimately our choice what we will make of it.

Physical affection that was constantly tempting Heidi and me during our engagement now takes work. This may sound strange to you single people, but sometimes it now takes a deliberate choice to hug Heidi or give her a kiss or a back rub. Don't get me wrong – I'm not saying these things have lost their pleasure or that I don't enjoy them. I do! It's just that there are so many other things – kids, work, projects, and goals – that distract me from my relationship with Heidi. For our love to flourish, I have to make deliberate, intentional choices.

However, just because true love isn't automatic doesn't mean it can't be found. I have seen examples of marriages that inspire me. My own parents have been married twenty-eight years and are more in love now than when they said "I do." Every summer, they go down to a cottage in Montana to celebrate their anniversary and they have to yank themselves away to go back home after a week of doing who-knows-what together. Even after eleven kids and all they have been through, their shared glance across the room still sizzles. In them, I see that lifelong romantic love is possible and very much worth fighting for.

Marriage can be the sweetest thing that ever happened to you, full of rich surprises and fantastic adventure. However, it can also be something that fills you, your spouse, and your children with pain and heartache. A bad marriage can be a terrible chain around your neck that will torment you for years.

Which kind of marriage will yours be? It's up to you.

The decisions you make in your single years will go a long way in determining the quality of your marriage. When you are young, long-term consequences may be the furthest thing from your mind; life is often focused on the next thrill. But your choices will affect your future. Wise decisions will bear delicious fruit that brings great delight. Foolish decisions can grow deep-rooted weeds that will choke and stab you for many years. A good marriage is possible, but it will take a lot of work and preparation. In this book I'd like to share with you some tools you need and steps you can take to make "happily-ever-after" a reality.

I want to inspire you single people to start investing right now in your future marriage relationship. Begin to do the hard work and you will reap huge benefits if God does lead you into a relationship. And even if He doesn't, you can still live "happily-ever-after" as a single person. The things we are suggesting will give you a solid foundation for an incredible, God-honoring marriage. But the reasons for building this strong foundation far exceed marriage. I believe that the actions and decisions that will form an excellent foundation for marriage are simply practical out-workings of obeying the greatest commandments – loving God and loving man. To obtain the riches of a relationship with God requires that we follow Christ's example of obedience to God's commands for life.

Our deepest need in life is not marriage. It is to regain fellowship with our Creator. Therefore, our ultimate goal in life should be to know God and obey His unique call for our life. A commitment to purity and self-sacrifice are the ingredients of a successful marriage, but a pursuit of these things is not a waste if God decides singleness is best for your life.

Our desire in writing this book is to equip young people for marriage, but this equipping should also be standard procedure for all who take the name of Christ. Your primary motivation for taking the steps this book suggests should be to obey and glorify your Creator. If your motivation for pursuing purity is merely so that you will have a better marriage, you'll be tempted to give in and compromise if God withholds marriage. If your only purpose for your single years is to prepare for marriage, then will your life become purposeless if marriage doesn't arrive?

Marriage is not the end purpose of life! Knowing and obeying God is. It is only when you get these priorities straight that marriage can become all that God wants it to be. Ironically then, your willingness to surrender to God the possibility of marriage may be the best way to prepare for it. That being said, the vast majority of you who are reading this book will someday get married, and I believe it's wise to live with an eye to the future, being aware of the consequences your actions will have on your possible future marriage and the future marriages of those with whom you interact.

There are so many lies that surround sex and love. Young people are falling for these lies and being robbed of the full delight that God has for them. Grave consequences can follow deception. If a young woman believes her drink is safe, she will go ahead and drink it. However, if that drink was spiked with a drug, awful consequences will follow. I believe Satan is taking the wonderful wine of love and spiking it so that what was supposed to be delightfully sweet now tastes of bitter heartache. I hope to expose some of these lies, so you can experience all that God wants to give you! I also want you to get a look at love, romance, and marriage from God's perspective rather than letting the culture define your views. Godly, zesty romances and marriages begin with a right perspective and understanding. Proper expectations will also go a long way to being prepared for true love.

We love talking about this wonderful gift and hope you will prayerfully consider the ideas we share about it. We're excited about these principles because we have found them to be very rewarding. Godly romance is so incredibly satisfying - it is truly worth the work.

A quick note about who wrote what in this book. I (Jesse) have written the majority of it. But every time Heidi contributes, her name will be noted in bold. It shouldn't be too confusing.

It is now our privilege to share with you the love story that God wrote for us. We enjoy turning the page each day to see what our loving Author has planned. We share this story not as a statement that you should do things the way we did, but to show you that when you put things in God's hand, you will be blessed. After our story, we would like to share some of the practical strategies we learned in the trenches while waiting for God to bring the right one along. God's got a blueprint for making true love. He holds out to you the tools and supplies. Now it's up to you to make true love a reality, so you too can experience extreme romance.

CHAPTER 1

OUR STORY: LOVE COMES LOUDLY

JESSE'S SIDE OF THE STORY

I am going to admit something right now that I never would have admitted while growing up with seven brothers: I am a romantic at heart. I love candlelit dinners and long moonlight strolls. I love spending time with the most beautiful woman who has ever walked the face of this planet – my wife, Heidi. In 2005, Heidi burst into my life with a brilliant blaze of color and changed me forever. I have fallen under her spell and hope to remain captive for life.

God made us to crave romance and the companionship of some special member of the opposite sex. While single, I dreamed – far more than I let on to my brothers – about how wonderful it would be to enjoy the companionship of a wife. Nights when I would baby-sit, after everyone else was asleep, I'd sit up in the living room and wish I had a wife to share this quiet moment with. Whenever we would meet a new family, my first thought was, "I wonder if they have a girl my age." I was always on the lookout for the future Mrs. Jesse Jost. My path to nuptial bliss was not what I expected (as you will read in the following pages), but what did prove true was that there is a good God who has shown time and time again that He can be trusted. As a young man, I committed to God my desire for a wife. He has blessed me beyond my imaginings.

I am the oldest of eleven children and I loved all that this distinction entailed. I changed diapers, enjoyed cooking, loved sporting and working with my seven brothers, and simply adored my little siblings. But even though I loved my family, I longed for the day when God would give me my own family, especially a kind-hearted and thoughtful woman with whom I could share my deepest thoughts and feelings.

Longing for marriage led to some mild heartache and disappointment. However, I tried to remember that since it was my Creator who made me with this desire, He would also fulfill this desire to the greatest degree. I also realized that these single years were a valuable time in a young man's life. I immersed myself in some of the great works of literature. I took several journeys through church history, examined different philosophies, studied numerous arguments for the truth of Christianity, and memorized much of the New Testament.

Through all this, I eagerly awaited the day when God would say, "The time has arrived! Come meet this beautiful bride that I have prepared for you!" There were a couple of times I excitedly thought this day was dawning, only to see the imaginary sun dissipate and awaken to the cold reality that it was still night and I should still be asleep. These experiences taught me humility and gave me a firm grasp of how deceptive human hearts can be.

LOVE AT FIRST SIGHT

When I was nineteen, I met – and was immediately attracted to – a girl who lived far away. I didn't care what James Dobson said; I suddenly believed in love at first sight. I'd grown up hearing that when my mom met my dad, she had the thought cross her mind, "I just met my future husband." I believed I was having a similar experience. I should have noted one key difference between Mom's experience and mine – this girl that I liked was beautiful and attraction to her was natural. On the other hand, when Mom and Dad met, Dad had yet to emerge from his gangly, geeky stage. Today, of course, Dad is a rugged, handsome hulk, but back then it had to be the voice of God giving Mom a thought like that.

Over the next year and a half, I prayed that God would give me this girl as my wife. I was really sincere about the whole thing, surrendering her to God and sharing my feelings about her with my mom. I prayed in a somewhat cowardly way, "God, if she's not the one you have for me, please take away this desire, but if she is the one, help this desire to grow." I thought it was a win-win prayer. If God took my desire away, there would be no disappointment if nothing came to fruition. I should have realized that we are responsible for directing and diligently guarding the desires of our heart instead of expecting God to do it for us. So rather than guard my heart, I followed my heart and found that my infatuation increased. I thought I was falling more and more in love.

The ridiculous thing was that I had only seen this girl a few times and really didn't know her. I have since discovered that it's easier to have crushes on people you don't know very well than on those you do. When you meet someone for the first time, huge unknown areas make up who that person is. It's like a lift-the-flap grid put over a picture. You flip back a flap at a time, trying to guess what the rest of the picture is like. It's similar in new relationships. You get to pull back a few flaps as you spend a little time together, revealing a bit of the other person's nature and character. We don't like living with unknown areas, though, so we often fill in the blanks ourselves, assuming things about the other person that may or may not be true. When a girl is outwardly attractive, it's easy to assume she is perfect and godly in other areas. (On the flip side, it's easy to be critical of a less attractive person's character.)

When we know a person really well after years of time together, many more of the flaps have been revealed and we see more of that person's faults and shortcomings. But with a new friend, there are still so many delicious blank spaces; our searching heart loves to imagine what lies behind that beautiful face.

I found this happening with me. This girl was beautiful and I assumed many things about her. I took her face, name, and the few things I had observed about her, entered these facts into my mental "create the perfect lover" program, and it filled in the rest of the picture with details I wanted to be true. Voila! A classic recipe for infatuation. I am not saying that this girl was not a wonderful person in real life, but rather that, in hindsight, I see I really didn't know her as well as I thought I did.

A CRUEL AWAKENING

Finally, after much prayer and waiting, my mom and dad suggested that I approach the young lady's father about beginning a relationship. So we went to visit their family. The first night we stayed there I was woken up by a little sibling who wet the air mattress we were sharing. I cleaned up the puddled mess but could not get back to sleep. Lying down on a big bean bag couch, I contemplated what I was about to do… and then the gravity of the situation hit me full force. My conviction was that when I started a romantic relationship I wanted it to be for life. I was not in this for casual fun; I was about to commit for life. It suddenly dawned on me how little I knew this girl. What was I in for? I tossed and turned and committed the whole thing again to God.

The next afternoon, with great fear and trepidation, I trembled up the stairs and into her father's office. He was on the phone and asked me to wait in the hall. "What am I doing?" I quivered. The young lady's father turned out to be very kind and relaxed. I poured out my heart, trying to persuade him that it was God who put this desire in my heart and that I would do my best to take care of his daughter. Graciously, he said he would pray about it with his wife and get back to me in two weeks. Immediately after the conversation, I was flooded with peace. I had been obedient and stepped out in faith. I felt like I was Abraham, George Mueller, and Hudson Taylor all rolled into one, and God was beginning one of the greatest love stories of all time. It seemed I had done everything right. Now it was just a matter of time. The two weeks were filled with apprehension, but by the end of the second week, I had a growing certainty. I was really excited.

Then the phone rang. It was the girl's father, and he wanted to talk to my dad first. Not a good sign. I talked with him a few minutes later. Actually, "talked" is too strong a description. It was more like I mumbled a few things while trying to get rid of the huge lump in my throat. With a few simple words, my fairytale train crashed abruptly into the face of rocky Heartbreak Mountain. It was over and I was stunned.

Was this some cruel cosmic prank? I had surrendered her to God, waited for confirmation from my parents, and now it was over! How could this be? Did this father have any idea that he'd just thrown to the wind a golden opportunity to guarantee his daughter's lifelong bliss? Did he know who he'd just turned down? I went downstairs to my bed and soaked the covers with tears. When I got up, I reached for "A Grief Observed" by C. S. Lewis. I thought maybe he knew how I felt. After reading his heart-wrenching account of real grief, I realized things weren't really all that bad. While it hurt my pride to be turned down and it was painful to have my expectations crushed, I was glad I had approached her father before starting a relationship. I had not communicated my affection to the girl and we had no shared romantic experiences so there were no soul ties to be severed. From what I have heard from others, that is when the real pain occurs.

A WOMAN OF MY (NOT) CHOOSING

Broken and humbled, I moved on. Ten months later, still feeling like a total failure in being able to read God's direction for love, I told my parents to choose a girl for me and that I would just learn to love whoever they picked. I know that decision may sound crazy, but I was beginning to realize that true love is a choice, something you cultivate and nourish. I now saw that there can only be infatuation at first sight, not true love. So I was willing to let them pick The Woman for me, trusting God to lead through them. My parents had been praying for my future spouse since the day I was born; I knew that they wanted what was best for me even more than I did.

They talked and prayed about it together and felt that there were two godly young women who were possibilities for me. One of them was someone I had been interested in before; the other one had not caught my fancy at all. They decided on the former, a young lady whom we all knew well. I had been attracted to her when I was younger, but had since totally died to that interest. Though I was not in love with her, I knew that, with time, I could be. But I was not joking when I said I had totally died to my desire for her. So when they told me who they had chosen, I had a sinking feeling in my chest. I was excited that my life would be moving forward, but struggled to wrap my head around this one. I stayed up till one in the morning praying and trying to turn my heart toward this girl. I felt like a noble martyr of love…with a case of nausea.

With slightly less apprehension, I called the girl's father and asked to begin a relationship with his daughter. He sounded positive at first, but decided to wait awhile before giving me permission. So for the next six weeks, I was learning to love the young lady my parents had chosen. It was beginning to work, too. The only problem was that the young lady's father was not getting back to me. I couldn't figure this out. When the opportunity of paradise for your daughter knocks on your door, why take so long to decide if you should let him in? Isn't it a no-brainer?

Eventually, the second father did decide: No. He said he really wanted to say yes, but he had no peace and was not getting any sleep. I began wondering if there were any monasteries for Protestants. Thankfully, I couldn't find any. But I did wonder if my strong desire for marriage would ever be fulfilled.

LOOK WHO'S AVAILABLE!

Shortly after false awakening # 2, I began to take more notice of a young lady in our church fellowship. She was the other girl my parents had thought was a good fit. They had suggested her to me before but in the past I had always rejected the idea. You see, I thought my cousin was interested in her. My cousin is about 6'1" and built like a lumberjack. I can make 5'10" with a good hair dryer, and am built for reading, so I wasn't about to get into a stag fight for her. I already had enough headaches in the love department. It turns out that my cousin was interested in this girl's younger sister and they had just announced their engagement a few months earlier. Their announcement opened up a new world of possibilities, and I had no idea just how wonderful this world would be!

I had always respected this slender, blond woman but could never figure out what she thought of me. I loved talking with her; she struck me as a very thoughtful person who listened carefully and weighed what was said without becoming defensive or argumentative. Nevertheless, even though my cousin was out of the way and The Girl was now available, I could not think of her as more than a friend – a possible great friend perhaps – but just a friend. Love was *not* my favorite topic any more.

Turning twenty-two had brought a dose of reality about all that marriage required, and that, much as I wanted to be married, I recognized that I would be unwise to try to manipulate things to make marriage arrive sooner. "Just trust God for His timing," I said to myself, for with His timing would come His grace. I decided the wisest thing to do would be to pursue my interest in writing, be open to more job opportunities, and be content right where God had me.

SHE LOVES ME, SHE LOVES ME NOT…SHE AT LEAST KNOWS I EXIST, RIGHT?

A growing fascination with this striking blonde led to more and more "coincidental" encounters with her. Our chats reinforced my belief that she would make an awesome friend, but I was still clueless about how she felt. I was pretty sure she didn't hate me! Beyond that, I couldn't figure her out.

In spite of everything, I could not ignore the increasing hold she had on me. I began to look forward to seeing her, and tried harder to arrange coincidental conversations, all the while seeking to convince myself she would just be a great friend. I started to keep an eye for any indication that she might view me as more than a friend, but alas, I could find none! I thought about approaching her father, but wanted to first make sure she was interested. I didn't want to finally get past the father only to be turned down by the girl!

In early June, I went hiking with a group of friends that included this particular young lady. I was eager to talk to her. I had recently begun writing an article for a periodical, and used it as an excuse to talk to this girl, who just happened to be a very talented writer. (A disclaimer to you guys: The pickup line, "I'm a writer, would you like to edit my work?" worked great for me, but it might not have the same effect on all girls.) The amazing thing about the hike was that I almost always found myself with *her!* She, on the other hand, appeared to be running away from me down the hill, forcing me to inauspiciously run after her. I couldn't figure out why she kept running away! "She wants me to follow her," I assured myself, proving once again that the male brain's version of logic is worthless when it comes to figuring out a female. At any rate, I loved every minute of talking to her. I found out later that during this hike my dad was praying that God would bring me and this young woman together if it was His will.

LOVE WRITTEN IN RED

The next day, our church had a Sunday school picnic. I could not fight my newfound attraction. I watched The Girl closely – I wanted her attention. Where I was concerned, the facade of "just friends" was gone. This change of heart resulted in frustration for me, because this girl would not give any hint of interest! I was confused. I knew where my heart wanted to go, but because it had led me wrong before, I tried to keep my desires in check and wait on the Lord. When I got home, I sent her the article I was working on. She promptly sent it back full of red ink. At this, I fell hopelessly in love. Not only was she beautiful, she also knew how to edit! What more could a man want?

With each passing week, I experienced a growing certainty that, if it was what God wanted, I would be thrilled to have this girl as my wife. My parents gave their approval when I shared my desire with them, but they also expressed a need for confirmation from the Lord and some indication that this young woman's heart was turning my direction. "Even if she isn't attracted to me now, she still could be the one!" I hedged.

Once again, I made the mistake of trying to interpret her actions using male logic. Was she blushing? Was she comfortable or uneasy around me? Was she looking at me? These questions yielded no answers. I knew as much as rocks do – nothing!

While I had no idea how she felt, I knew how I felt! I couldn't get her off my mind. One evening, on August 12, 2005, I sensed I had clear confirmation from the Lord: Yes, she's the one for you. I was instantly excited, but I quickly tempered my soaring emotions by reminding myself that one's thoughts tend to be deceitful and mine had deceived me before. Still, it seemed clear. I prayed that God would unmistakably direct in this situation. God had showed me in the past that if something wasn't His will, He could protect me from it.

I felt I needed to approach her father. Having gone through the pain of being turned down in the past, I was reluctant to do so now. I had to be sure this was God's will before venturing down that difficult road again!

She what?!

God sure knows how to surprise us! The young woman's parents contacted my parents about meeting together for coffee. Because they live a hundred miles away from us, the get-together was not some casual suggestion. Mom suspected that it might have something to do with their daughter. I went for a walk with Mom the night before the parents' meeting and once again shared exactly where my heart was, but also said the future looked so uncertain.

I left early for work the next day (Tuesday, Aug. 23), anxiously awaiting news about the meeting. Shortly after 11 a.m., I got a call at work from Mom. She relayed the conversation, sharing that the girl's parents started things off by saying they had noticed how much attention I was giving their daughter, Heidi, and were concerned about it. My heart sank. Oh no, not again! Strike three.

"They wanted to know where your heart was," Mom continued, "because" – her next words jolted my mind with a rush of joy – "Heidi has believed you were the one for her for six to eight months!!!" I discovered then what it was like to lose touch with reality. My head was in the clouds

– I ran on air all the way to cloud nine!

"Heidi has so much respect for you," Mom said. "She just thinks the world of you!" I simply could not believe what I was hearing! I finally knew what ecstasy felt like: I'm twenty-two and for the first time in my life I know that a girl likes me!

LIFE IN THE CLOUDS

I hung up the phone in a daze. I couldn't stop grinning. In my delirium that afternoon I ran into a combine – which is different from a concubine – on my way home from work. There were four in a row coming down the gravel road toward me. I missed the first two, but the third one's header hit the corner of the windshield and scraped along the roof. This temporarily dampened my enthusiasm, as this was my brother's car I was driving. (He later sold it to me at a reduced rate.) But not even a damaged windshield could keep my spirits down.

The next morning I experienced two firsts – writing my first love letter and filing my first police report. The love letter is more interesting, so I'm including it here.

> *My beautiful and lovely Heidi,*
> *I am so totally excited and overjoyed at the sudden turn of events that God has brought into our lives. As you may have noticed, I have gradually been falling madly in love with you. (Despite the fact that, frustratingly, I had no idea how you felt… I was pretty sure you didn't hate me!) When Mom called me at work, telling me about the visit and how you felt, I was rocketed to cloud nine, I felt like I was on top of the world, the luckiest man alive! (Please overlook all the clichés. I will work hard on avoiding them in future letters!) I had a big goofy grin on my face for hours. I would try and sober up before asking someone a question, and then I would go back to my work and just grin!*
> *I had a great talk with your parents last night. They are awesome people that I already love dearly! They have given me permission to ask you if it would work to take you on a walk Friday afternoon. I hope you will say yes. I am so excited about talking to you and pouring out my heart! I am simply overwhelmed with God's goodness that He would honor me with such a gem as you. I can't wait to start sharing life with you, growing closer to God with you, and together enjoying the great adventures He has in store for us.*
> *I LOVE YOU, Heidi Wahl!*
> *Love, your not-so-secret admirer, Jesse Jost*

I had it delivered to her as she was staying at some friends in the area and waited for her reply. On Thursday morning I received the first of hundreds of special emails from Heidi:

> *YES! Any time on Friday afternoon works GREAT! - I don't know what else to say... Jesse, I don't even feel like I'm me anymore, and I'm not sure what daydream I just walked into, or who I'm sharing it with, or why this happened to me of all people. I don't know which way is up right now, and seeing you - talking to you - would straighten it all out. You have always straightened things out for me, seems like, ever since I first met you. And I can't wait to tell you what God has done over the past year! He is amazing! I am so in awe of His love - open-hearted, unreserved love. Like yours. I don't deserve either, can't comprehend either!*
>
> *Don't examine and re-examine this email, please, Jess. I'm not sure what to say or how to say it just now and my words are clumsy. There are a million things I want to say, but email isn't the place for it. I just need to see you and be reassured that you are the same person I have always looked up to and appreciated, and then maybe the reality of all of this will begin to settle in!*

Learning to love,
    Heidi

CAUGHT IN LOVE'S OVERWHELMING FLOW

Contrary to what she said, I did read that letter over and over and over. It is hard to describe the rush of emotions I was feeling. It was like I entered some kind of alternate reality. Friday morning, (August 26, 2005) I finished up a job and then, with fluttering insides, drove to meet Heidi. After pondering what I would say first, I stepped out of the car, and walked toward Heidi, who was sitting on the lawn in front of her sister's house. Ultra-smooth, I began, "Nice day, isn't it?"

I sat down beside her and handed her some gifts. Every member of my family had written her a note welcoming her to the family, so I gave those to her. I had also bought her a white gold necklace with a ring through a heart.

"It symbolizes that my heart is yours forever," I said, and bashfully looked away. My metamorphosis from he-man to soggy milksop toast was underway.

On that hot sunny afternoon, Heidi and I officially began our relationship with an eight-hour conversation. I shared my heart, which had already been obvious to Heidi, and then Heidi shared part of her journal with me. I sat dumbfounded to hear this account of her long-time interest in me. She read how she became convinced that I was the man for her. She read of her struggles to surrender me to the Lord and how difficult it was to see me on Sundays... and how difficult it was when I wasn't there. She read of her growing certainty that I was the one she was going to marry. I was blown away!

We began our relationship that day with commitment to marriage. I told her that I had received the green light from God, my parents, and her parents, and that I was committing to marriage. No matter what, I would not back out of this relationship. I did tell her that if she found something in me that she did not like, she could back out. She refused the offer and committed to me as well.

This commitment soon became important to the health of our young relationship. I let loose twenty-two years of pent-up emotion. This emotional outburst – I wore out my exclamation point key in my e-mails to her – put the brakes on her falling in love with me. But because we were committed, we didn't panic; we worked it out and I learned the proper way to win a woman's heart. Hint: The best way to cause a delicate flower to blossom is not to spray it with a pressure hose.

To propose to her, I'd carved out a ring-box-sized hole in a big green book entitled "Life Begins" and took her for a walk. I handed her the book and watched as she flipped though the first few pages. I wanted her to get further back where the ring was, so I said, "I think chapter ten was a good one."

She found the ring and said, "Would you put it on?" I shakily slipped it on her finger. Twenty-four hours later, I worked up enough courage to hold her hand for the first time. The first time either of us had held hands, actually... in a romantic sense, of course! Those who have been initiated know the difference between holding hands and holding hands - much different from the family prayer circle! *Wow!* Six months later we shared our first kiss immediately following our wedding vows.

God is so good! There have been so many times I have looked at Heidi and been flooded with gratitude that those two previous fathers turned me down. God showed me that He is sovereign and that when I surrendered the choice of my lifelong spouse to Him, He lovingly ensured that I would marry the woman He had for me. I love her more than I can say.

HEIDI'S SIDE OF THE STORY

Heidi: I feel like Rembrandt plopped one of his masterpiece paintings in my arms, and I want to yell after him, "Please come back here and take another look at me. Double-check. Are you sure you've got the right person, sir?!" I am so unworthy of Jesse, and so in awe of God for this gift that has come in spite of – well, in spite of ME.

A CUT ABOVE THE REST

Jesse caught my attention the first time I visited his church (December 2002). That Sunday morning as he shared some insights from the Bible, his simple, wise words instantly won my respect. I saw that this guy had rare qualities: discernment and maturity beyond his years. He stood out even more when contrasted with the guys I'd been around at Bible school for the past few months. This night and day difference got me curious to learn more about what made Jesse such a great guy. When I found out that he liked books, boy, was I hooked. But my shy and retiring nature held me back from pummeling Jesse with questions. So, I kept my ears and eyes open. I heard good reports about Jesse from various friends - how he served his family selflessly and how he spent so much time in disciplined study of the Bible. Sunday after Sunday, I saw for myself how he reached out to others in love and compassion, with well-seasoned words. I was all agog, but not in love yet.

The Lord had work to do – still does! – however, in honing my focus on Him and His will. In order to do that, He had to remove some things that were cluttering my way to Christ-likeness. Okay, I'll drop the vague and go specific. I was really discontent at home, and wishing for some kind of thrilling, center-stage work to do. Jesse seemed pretty content at home. How'd he get that attitude? And how, in a world where men are expected to leave home right away to learn a trade, did he find the purpose to stay back, juggling studying with serving his family? Jesse's example fueled in me a desire to please God. He knew God's standard in purity, faith, love, and speech and proceeded to live by it. Without realizing it at first, I was increasingly drawn to the freedom and joy I saw in his life.

Time went by. The good reports about Jesse kept coming, and I kept filing them in my memory. People instinctively looked up to and turned to Jesse for wise counsel. Maybe he didn't see this, but I sure did! I began to wish that I could get to know him better and find out for myself what was going on inside his active mind. But I was also intimidated by his great, though humble, knowledge of spiritual things, and I believed that if we got to talking together more, he'd find out what a pompous ignoramus I was, and – well, that would be the end of that! Or so I thought. Still, I couldn't get him off my mind. There were times that I would be reading a book and come across some new idea that made me wonder, "What would Jesse think of this?" Or I would be seeking to share Christ with some stranger, and when they threw out an argument against Christianity, I'd ask myself, "What would Jesse say?"

When summer 2004 rolled around, I admitted it. I liked Jesse. And I liked him a whole lot more than the passel of other guys I'd been infatuated with.

GROWING UP

While I got ready to leave for a two and a half month-long music tour with a Christian family, my younger sister started courting another guy from our church. Yeah, the cousin Jesse was talking about. Perhaps it was Rebecca's courtship that really increased my own desire for marriage and for Jesse. I don't know. But leaving on that tour was one of the hardest things I ever did. I took with me a verse that straightened out my focus again and again as the weeks of the tour passed by: "He who trusts in his own heart is a fool, but whoever walks wisely will be delivered." Proverbs 28:26. I see more clearly now the necessary lessons God began to teach me during my time away from home - lessons that are now a huge blessing in my relationship with Jesse: open communication, frequent encouragement, and transparent honesty. Though I had started out the tour with tears, I finished it with a heart full of gratitude to God for changing me to become a little more like Him. All He wanted was for me to trust Him so that He could do more of His perfect work in me.

My tune in December was: Home again, home again, jiggety-jig - yahoo! I was excited to see Jesse again, and also excited to see God change certain areas of my life. I purposed to work harder at being encouraging and open with my family. For the first time, I began to truly give my heart to my dad by confiding in him my questions, doubts, struggles, and anxieties about a lot of matters. And as I did, I experienced more security than I ever had before. Daddy started asking me on Sundays, "So how did it go with Jesse today?" And I would answer, "Fine - great - not-so-good - it was tough - I don't know," depending on what had happened that day. I can't describe fully to you how protected and secure I felt during this time, knowing that Daddy was looking out for me, and feeling free to talk to him about whatever was on my mind.

Somehow, without my initiating anything, Jesse and I started talking a lot more. I would go home and analyze each conversation: Now did he answer this way because he's interested, or was he just being friendly, like Daddy says?

I grew tired of the inner conflict of warding off thoughts about Jesse, and I finally decided that instead of suppressing these thoughts, (which was purt' near impossible) I would take them captive by turning them into prayers for Jesse: Lord, make him Yours completely. Teach him to love You better than anything and anyone else. Increase his hunger for You and protect him from impurity and worldly wisdom. Feeling both confident and foolish, I wrote in my journal, "I want to marry Jesse." But I didn't know where Jesse's heart was in relation to me, so I went on analyzing and guessing: Did the guy even want to get married? Or was he oblivious to the world of girls? In his interactions with young ladies, he was always so careful about protecting their hearts and his own. Sunday encounters with Jesse continued to be enjoyable – and difficult; our friendship was great, but I wanted more than friendship.

WAITING IMPATIENTLY

The famous June hike showed me where things seemed to be with Jesse; I could tell that his heart was turning toward me. And the verse that had guarded my own heart – what was I to do with that now? He who trusts in his own heart is a fool, but he who walks wisely will be delivered. That night after the hike, I turned this verse over and over in my mind, and finally came to the conclusion that maybe it was possible for me to have this desire for Jesse, and still walk wisely.

As my certainty about him grew, so did my impatience. Late one night, I sat at the kitchen table with my parents (poor them! - they listened to so many of my heart palpitations!), and poured out my frustration and impatience about having to wait for something to happen. Everything seemed ready - set - but no go! What was up with that?! I was sure that "Jesse + me" was God's will. So why was it taking so long for Him to get this good thing going? Daddy remarked that my unpeaceful spirit was not a sign of contentment; his gentle words cut deeply. I felt awful that I hadn't trusted the wisdom of the Giver of all good things, and I repented there at the kitchen table. Then - and only then - God began to give me peace, and an incomprehensible contentment.

When our family took an August holiday, I had a lot of time to journal – and to think. Most of my thoughts were about Jesse, and so were my journal entries, "Now I believe I have freedom to write another statement, borne out of a growing desire: I will marry Jesse. And soon. Probably within a year. I am willing to wait now - not forever (that is too great a weight, under any circumstance, for anyone to bear), but one day at a time. It is always happier that way, anyhow, to get a thing in God's time." In hindsight, I see how easy it was to write such a prophetic statement, because I was feeding off my own desire and my strong (narcissistic?) assurance that Jesse was interested in me, too.

COULD I LIVE WITHOUT HIM?

The Saturday after we got back from our holiday, I went on an afternoon river tubing trip with a group of young people from our church. Jesse managed to keep his tube near mine the whole time, so we talked a lot as we floated down the river. That night I tossed restlessly in bed, turning memories of the day over and over in my mind. I kept thinking, too, about something my sister had said, "I've heard you shouldn't marry the person you think you can live with, but rather the person you can't live without." Then she asked me: "Can you live without Jesse?" She said that if I didn't think I could, then it was a pretty clear indicator that he was the man God had for me. Problem was, I could honestly answer "yes" to that question. Yes, I could live without Jesse as my husband. I could even live without him as a good friend. I felt guilty about this conclusion. Did this mean I was fickle and didn't care as much as I thought I did? Or did it mean God had somebody else for me?

Eventually I realized that my sister's well-meaning question was flawed, not my answer. With relief, I fell asleep in the security that whether or not Jesse was part of my future, I knew God would be sufficient for me. I couldn't live without God, but by His grace, I could handle it if He didn't bless me with Jesse as my life companion.

GETTING THINGS OUT IN THE OPEN

The next day, Sunday, August 21, my dad came to me after we'd gotten home from church, and said, "That Jesse sure was obvious today!"

I nodded. Our church had met at a riverside park for worship, and the whole hot afternoon, it seemed like Jesse had been wangling ways to talk to me. In the few times he wasn't nearby, it sure looked like he wanted to be. Then again, maybe that was my ego reading into things a bit, and assuming he was like everybody else – just perishing to hang out with Heidi. I was chatting with my friend Ashley before we left for home, and then Jesse joined us. He asked Ashley a question, but interrupted her answer to ask me something. Ashley gave us both a funny look. I was delighted beyond description: this incredible guy liked me and liked talking to me! But I was also unsure what to do about it, because if this kept up, more than just Ashley might start to notice. Why hadn't Jesse approached my parents yet? I'd been hoping for that.

I sensed approval not only from Jesse, but also from his parents... which just sent me through the roof with joy at the possibility! A week earlier, his mom mentioned to me that they were going to an outdoor symphony performance, and it would be so fun to take me with them, but "people would probably wonder," she smiled. I thought there was a question in her expression: Was there anything on my end? Was I interested? I didn't have a clue what to say, so I said nothing and tried not to show anything either. Which wasn't exactly helpful to Jesse or his parents.

Now back to my dad and his observation: "Jesse was sure obvious today!" Daddy went on to say that he felt the Time Had Come to talk to Mr. and Mrs. Jost. He'd suggested this several times before, explaining that he could just let them know I was interested in Jesse and ask them to pray about it. Till now, I always vehemently refused. I did not want to go down in history as the girl who basically went to her future husband's parents with a marriage proposal. I already had a reputation, earned or otherwise, in my family for being independent-minded and strong-willed; I didn't want to add to that image. Because I really, really desired to clearly see God's will regarding Jesse and me, I tried to step out of the way by not flirting or showing any especial interest in Jesse. I didn't want to tweak things in my favor. I had no idea that my unreadable behavior was part of the reason Jesse hadn't talked to my dad yet. I figured Jesse was the kind of guy who would be upfront with a girl's parents about his love-interest, so I was surprised – with all the attention he'd shown me – that he hadn't followed it up with a talk with my parents.

But now I felt like things had come to a head, and something needed to be done about Jesse's interest and mine. So I told Daddy it was okay by me if he and Mama talked to Jesse's parents and asked them what his intentions were, because I wanted to know. If Mr. and Mrs. Jost asked whether I was interested, too, I told Daddy he was welcome to tell them... I figured that was better than just volunteering the information.

Since I had made plans to visit friends who lived near Josts, Daddy and Mama took me north with them and dropped me off on the edge of the town golf course before going to meet Josts for coffee. It was a warm, mellow day, and I fell asleep by the eighth hole. When I woke up, an older lady was standing by her cart, looking at me with concern. She said, "Are you okay?"

I answered, "Oh yeah, just enjoying the day..." And waiting for my future to be decided, I added mentally.

How wonderful to hear those incredible words: "Jesse is interested in you, and believes you're the woman God has for him to marry!" The day after Jesse's parents met with mine, I wrote, "I am at an awe-filled loss for words. What a God, what a God! I can't comprehend the half of this gift, these circumstances, this amazing man who wants to marry me."

OVERWHELMED AND WEIRDED OUT

Mixed with the awe of having my dreams of Jesse fulfilled, I felt awkward and, for awhile, pulled back my emotions into a shell. Jesse wasn't sure what to make of me, nor was I of him. In my eyes, he turned into this impassioned lover, spilling over with words of love. I didn't know what to do with that. Where did the Jesse I was familiar with go? – the Jesse I loved to talk with about books? Was his exclamation point key on his computer stuck, or did he really feel all that overflow of love for little ol' me? I'd never had much attention from guys before (a good thing for me, who was ready to become infatuated at the drop of a hat), and all of a sudden, here was this good, godly, pure-hearted man who apparently adored me and thought I was the most awesome woman ever. I was pretty shell-shocked. It's one thing to hope and dream of marrying the guy and to have all those feelings lived out in the la-la-land of my mind, but when the dream becomes reality, there's some adjustment I didn't expect. Yeah, yeah, fickle, bizarre female emotions, I know.

There's something I wished I'd thought of at the beginning of Jesse's and my relationship, when I was feeling really weirded out and overwhelmed. I wish I'd realized that the emotions I was feeling would settle down in time – such as being nervous about marriage, or feeling hesitant to share myself with another person I didn't really know, or wondering what was wrong with me and why I wasn't more excited or acting more myself. Before I even saw Jesse for our first date (after we knew this thing was a "go"), someone counseled me to just be open with Jesse about everything I was thinking and feeling. That was some of the worst advice I got. Later on, when we were more comfortably settled into who each other was, that would have been wonderful advice. But at the beginning, when I was overwhelmed with all these new emotions and didn't know how to handle them, I followed the advice I was given and ended up saying things that really weren't me. For example, I told Jesse emphatically that I was a "no-touchy-touch" girl (just because I was nervous about physical affection), and I also said that I hated flowers as a romantic gift – stuff like that. So Jesse was quite confused for awhile about who I really was; I gave him a conflicting picture with my emotionally driven statements. I have changed a lot as time passed. Obviously.

Anyway, in the midst of confusing emotions, I came to recognize that I would eventually return to the person I was. As it turned out, I kept a lot of my feelings to myself for the first couple of months and just held out on the waves I was riding. I finally figured that I didn't have to have an explanation for everything I felt... I could go ahead and just feel it, and then give it to God, and realize with relief that things would settle down and I'd really start falling in love with Jesse. And, boy, did I ever! It helped so much to look back at the confirmations God had given me up to the start of our relationship, and remember that yes, Jesse was the one God had chosen for me, and the man I had committed to that day in August. My parents' and his parents' approval was also a huge, huge confirmation and such a strength to lean on.

MY HERO!

Back in February 2005, Jesse and I went on a day trip with several friends, and as we were heading home, somebody suggested that we say something encouraging about the person on our left. Jesse turned out to be my "encouragement assignment." I was so glad for that, because I'd long wanted to tell him how much God had used him to challenge me. I quoted the verse that I'd often thought of in relation to Jesse and his influence on me: Be imitators of me, just as I also am of Christ.

So that's pretty much the sum of it: I am thrilled to spend the rest of my life with Jesse, following his example, and through it, loving God more!

LIFE BEGINS

Jesse: We were married on March 25th, 2006 – exactly seven months after our relationship began. Our engagement days were wonderful, but they were filled with ups and downs. Saving your first kiss for marriage is very hard on the neck muscles when you are as in love as Heidi and I were. (The magnetic pull put lots of extra strain on the muscles) We had to work through different issues and expectations that we had, but it was so wonderful to have that security of commitment while dealing with the challenges that are inherent in romantic love. The month before our wedding I wrote a song for Heidi. I surprised her and sang it to her for the first time just before our first kiss. I think the lyrics are a fitting conclusion to our story.

YOURS ALONE

Words by Jesse Jost
Music by Lisa Jost

Darling, as long as we can breath, I will never love another,
I will always be here for you my bride, in my arms you can take cover.

(chorus)
I am yours and yours alone; it will always be this way,
I lay down my life for you this day, by His grace, I am yours alone.

Beloved, my eyes are yours alone, your beauty's enough for me,
I will always delight myself in you, you are all I want to see.

Because my God owns all of me, I can give myself to you,
His almighty grace, is sufficient and free, He alone can make this true.

CHAPTER 2

GOD'S DESIGN FOR LIFELONG ROMANCE

God loves to give His children good gifts! His creativity, wisdom, and love manifest themselves in the varied pleasures He bestows on us. But as with any gift, there is a right way and a wrong way to enjoy it. We can maximize the enjoyment of the gift or misuse it so badly that it actually becomes a curse. With each gift comes a responsibility to not let it go to waste or to use it improperly.

Suppose your parents give you the sports car of your dreams. You are blown away! This is the most awesome gift you have ever been given. However, the car comes with some strict rules: you must only fill up the tank with gasoline, you have to make sure that the fluid levels are topped up and that you don't run the engine dry, not to mention that you also have to follow the rules of the road.

At this point, you have two choices. You can say, "This is my sports car and I can do whatever I want with it." Or you can decide to submit to the regulations. Now imagine that you decide to treat the car any way you please. You put diesel in the gas tank, you ignore the oil light, and you run it hard even though you are low on coolant. Where will that "freedom" lead? A sports car engine needs the proper fuel and coolant or it will cease to run. It may be your car, but this does not change the fact that if certain conditions are not followed, the car will quit working and you'll be left with a lifeless hunk of metal.

Or let's say you decide that the sports car would make a really cool tree house, so you hoist it up in a tree. Such an idea may be enjoyable, but you would be completely missing out on the true power and potential of the sports car. To maximize your enjoyment of the sports car, you need to know its real purpose.

In the case of a sports car, what constitutes real freedom? Making any choice you want? Using the gift for whatever you desire? Is it being stuck high in a tree or stalled in traffic? Or is the real freedom found in restricting yourself to the rules laid down for you and having a powerful car that will enable you to cruise the highways wherever you want to go? Do you see how the rules are not restrictive, but are instead empowering? In the same way, God's rules for the gifts that He gives us are for our pleasure, enabling us to find the gift's real potential.

Romantic love and physical intimacy are amazing gifts with the capacity to bring great pleasure and fulfillment. But they come with "For best results…" and "Caution: do not…" labels. Love and sex were designed to operate best under certain guidelines and conditions. If these instructions are followed you can enjoy these gifts to the fullest. However, if you ignore the Designer's instructions and misuse His gifts, they won't function the way they were designed to. God's instructions are to keep romantic love and sex in the context of lifelong commitment. This may seem strange or radical to you, but God's instructions serve to ensure that His carefully crafted engines of sex and romantic love run smoothly. Let's take a closer look at love and romance and ways to maximize their horsepower.

COMMITMENT AND ROMANCE

Any realistic view of love needs to make a distinction between the choice to love (commitment) and the feelings of love (romance). Like all emotions, the feelings of love will come and go no matter how strong they seem to be. But committed love is an unchanging choice. To really love your wife or your husband is a choice, not a mere feeling. True love says, "I will stay faithful to you no matter how I feel. I will serve, protect, honor, and cherish you even when the feelings go." When a couple wants a divorce because they "no longer love each other," they are demonstrating ignorance about what true love really is. True love is not something that you verify is there by taking emotional inventory. Rather, it is a decision you make. Marriage is a vow before God to stay committed to loving your spouse till death separates you. This vow does not say that "I will have feelings for you always, but that I will always choose to serve you and stay faithful to you."

That being said, the feelings of love are not unimportant. God has given us an incredible gift in these feelings of romantic love and physical intimacy, overflowing with pleasure almost too great to comprehend. But, like the sports car, this gift is not a mere toy to be enjoyed any way you please. And just as the sports car has a functional job of transportation, the gift of erotic love has the function of cementing lifelong commitment in marriage and developing genuine intimacy.

ROMANTIC SUPERGLUE

Physical affection and romantic love are powerful adhesives that bond a man and a woman together and make them one. Things such as hand holding, kissing, long intimate one-on-one conversations of pouring your heart out and sharing your deepest dreams and fears, love notes, and romantic dates – these are all ingredients of the romantic glue that pulls a couple together. The more these activities are enjoyed, the stronger the bond between young people grows.

Much is made of the bonding that happens in the sex act, but serious bonding happens in all romantic activity. It is not just through intercourse that your souls begin to adhere and form soul ties. There is emotional and spiritual bonding that happens through the expressions of romantic love. When couples start to see themselves as "an item" and have a shared identity, they are acknowledging the welding of their souls.

God designed the glue of erotic love to be permanent: One man and one woman cemented for life (Mark 10:6-9). Listen to any love song, or overhear any lovers' conversation and you'll find that they are full of promises to forget all others and stay faithful forever. Lovers love to promise forever. That is the way God intended it to be. Any person who has been through a breakup knows the horrendous pain it brings. It hurts because the love-glue holding these young people together was designed to hold forever. Hearts bonded with romantic-erotic love glue cannot separate cleanly; they will inevitably break and tear.

Not only does the breakup tear the heart and cause pain, but a callus will form on the wound, making it harder to bond to someone else next time. Or think of it this way: Our hearts are like a sticky piece of tape; the first time it is applied to a surface, it sticks very well and is hard to remove. But when it's pulled away, it becomes less sticky. The more the tape is applied and removed, the less sticky it becomes.

Sadly, young people have been taught that it's normal and healthy to enter into several romantic relationships before marriage, and that kissing, hand holding, long heart-to-heart talks, and love notes are all harmless parts of young love. But these young men and women are playing with superglue – stuff far more powerful than they realize. They are bonding and breaking many times before marriage. They are scraping and tearing their tender hearts because they don't know any other way to love. And millions of them are paying the consequences, not only in the pain and heartache of breakups, but with a lessening "stickiness." The calluses on their hearts are making it more difficult to bond permanently. It is no wonder that the divorce rate is so high. How God must weep to see His wonderful gift so abused. Because of the lies they believe, many people never get to discover just how wonderful God-designed love can be.

Thankfully, there is a better way. But it requires a radical shift away from the world's thinking.

GOD'S WORD ON ROMANCE
If you want God's best, then you will make Christ the Lord of

your love life and seek absolute purity. I want to be clear and upfront that I don't simply want to sit here and spout a lot of rules and laws that you have to follow. Rather, I am trying to look at God's ideal for love and romance and inspire you to seek God as to what is the best way to submit your love life to His design. There are so many beliefs that the culture and media are feeding us. Some of these beliefs are false and it's easy to swallow them uncritically and end up being led astray.

Each age has its blind spots. Many people growing up in the South during the early 1800s thought nothing of treating African-Americans like animals. When slave-holders consulted the Bible for guidance, they discovered that there was no verse explicitly stating that slavery was wrong or that blacks should have equal rights with whites, so they assumed that this was a grey area and they didn't need to worry further about it. In the meantime, millions of blacks were suffering the terrible consequences of these wrong beliefs. The Abolitionists looked at the biblical text a little more carefully, listened to the spirit of the law, and followed biblical passages to their logical conclusion to form their convictions. They saw that all men were created in the image of God and were therefore equal (Genesis 1:26 and Job 31:13-15). Paul saw slaves as brothers and sisters in Christ (1 Timothy 6:2). The Abolitionists also realized that the way we treat other humans is the way we treat Christ (Matthew 25:40). From these passages, they drew the accurate conclusion that slavery was wrong and that it should be abolished.

Today, of course, we recognize that the views of slaveholders were wrong and damaging. But back then, overturning the majority mindset on slavery required people who were willing to question the accepted norms and see if they lined up with God's revealed principles. I want you to do the same thing and re-examine some of our culture's assumptions about love and romance and prayerfully consider some ideas that at first you may find radical.

When it comes to determining right and wrong in our romantic relationships, God has not spelled out in specific detail exact boundaries or clearly defined how far is too far. However, He has given us some straightforward principles that we can apply to these areas. Much of what I suggest in this book comes from these biblical guidelines.

1. When God designed marriage, He only included one man and one woman (Genesis 1-2).

2. When a couple comes together in marriage, God designed their bond to be permanent (Mark 10:6-9).

3. God tells us to abstain from all sexual immorality (Acts 15:20; 1 Corinthians 6:18, 10:8; 1 Thessalonians 4:3). This includes fornication

(sexual immorality before marriage) and adultery (sexual immorality after marriage with someone other than your spouse). In Ephesians 5:3, Paul tells us, "But among you there must not be even a hint of sexual immorality, or of any kind of impurity, or of greed, because these are improper for God's holy people." (NIV) By consulting your conscience, seeking the Holy Spirit, and looking at erotic love from a few different angles, I believe God will make clear what He means by "sexual immorality."

4. Impurity involves more than overt acts; it starts with and includes our thoughts (Matthew 5:28).

5. God specifically commands us to not defraud each other in the area of sexual immorality (1 Thessalonians 4:6). Defrauding happens when you promise something and don't pay up, or you create false expectations and don't come through. I think single people defraud each other when they begin bonding to each other in a romantic way outside the safety of marriage commitment. Romantic involvement implies permanence and if one or both young people are not willing to commit, they are misleading each other. By doing so, they're not only causing future pain in the person they are defrauding, but they are also stealing from that person's future spouse.

6. We are to love our wives like Christ loves the church (Ephesians 5:25). This kind of love, I believe, includes fidelity to her during and before marriage.

7. All of our relationships should be governed by agape love (I Corinthians 13), which means that we should put the needs of others (including our future spouse) ahead of our own (Philippians 2:4).

8. God loves to see sex and erotic love enjoyed in the proper boundaries of marriage – just read Song of Solomon.

I think we can glean some guidelines for our romantic relationships by reasoning from these principles.

ONE MAN. ONE WOMAN.

God designed romantic love to be exclusively between one man and one woman. When you add another man or woman to the equation it results in damage far greater than putting diesel in a gasoline engine. This is not just some arbitrary social invention, but a law of nature that cannot be violated without doing harm. The addition of a third party into romance creates problems with jealousy, insecurity, suspicion, guilt, withdrawal, feeling compared and criticized.

Most people try to follow this one-man-woman, one-woman-man rule after they enter marriage. They abstain from entering a romantic relationship with someone who is not their spouse and would find it wrong to hold hands with another woman, or kiss another man, or go out for a long, romantic, candlelit dinner, because they want to stay faithful to their spouse. But what people often don't realize until it's too late is that infidelities to your spouse before marriage can be just as damaging to your relationship as infidelities that happen after marriage.

When you do something romantic with another person, your action exists for all time. You can't change the past. The tape of what you did is playing somewhere for all eternity, and that act can keep popping up in your memory. The things you do become a part of who you are. Many people refuse to kiss another woman after they are married, but when you kiss another woman before marriage it is just as wrong because it's something you can't change. Memories of that kiss will haunt you and your spouse because that kiss is a part of you. You have added an intruder that will mess up the sacred formula of one plus one that profound intimacy requires.

What I'm saying may sound ridiculous to some, but really, it's not that far off from what most people believe. Even young people who enter casual romantic premarital relationships expect that the person they are in the relationship with shouldn't be doing romantic stuff with anybody else. If the other person was caught holding hands or snuggling with someone else, they would call it cheating. We feel this need for exclusivity in love very strongly, and we are hurt when it's broken.

For romance to operate at optimum levels, it requires more than just "one lover at a time" – rather, "one lover for life." If you think this sounds too restrictive or too narrow-minded, remember the sports car. Filling the car's tank with only gasoline – is that restrictive? You bet! But it's also the only way the car will run smoothly because that's how it was designed. So, too, with romance: The engine of love that was purring like a kitten on the clean fuel of exclusivity will start to howl and back fire if you add the foreign substance of infidelity.

When you are romantic and physical with a person outside of commitment, your actions can take on a life of their own and become an enemy that will continue to torment you for life and rob you of the fullness of bliss that could be yours. What you do becomes an indelible part of who you are.

I am jealous for my wife, past, present, and future. Even past interests that she had slightly bother me, but what thrills me to no end and makes me want to shout hallelujah is that she has no romantic ties with any other guy! I could time-travel through her life and never feel uncomfortable with the way that she interacted with other guys.

THE BLAZING FIRES OF PASSIONATE ROMANCE

The feelings of erotic love are powerful, consuming fires. The commitment to lifelong fidelity (marriage) provides the necessary framework to keep these fires under control. The pioneers had a saying that fire was a wonderful servant but a terrible master. When fire is under control, it can cook your food, provide warmth, and create a delightful atmosphere on a cold winter night. However, when this same fire gets out of control it can be devastating. Five years ago, some close friends of ours, a family with nine children, got a call two days before Christmas that their house was on fire. They rushed back only to find the place engulfed in flames. Everything was lost. The fire that was so useful and pleasurable when confined brought such terrible devastation when it got out of control.

Song of Solomon 8:6 says love "burns like a blazing fire, like a mighty flame." (NIV) In the context of commitment, the fires – or feelings – of love can be more pleasurable than you can imagine. But when they are allowed to burn freely and take control of you, much that is precious to you can be lost in the flames.

Romantic passion can put an absolute spell over you, making wrong seem right and convincing you that the only thing that matters in life is being with your special mate. From the outside looking in, it is obvious that a couple claiming to be madly in love, even though they have known each other for just a few days, are only experiencing infatuation. It can't be true love because they don't know each other; their love hasn't been tested.

But when you are on the inside, you may only see that, right now, your feelings are so strong you both just have to be right for each other. And as long as you let this fire that you feel for your lover be the driving force of your life, it won't matter to you what your family thinks, what God thinks, what life purpose you neglect, or what beliefs you previously held. The fires of romance have destroyed marriages, stolen girls from loving homes and made them heartbroken and destitute, robbed young men of their passion to serve God, and left children weeping.

Because of the misuse of these God-given desires and feelings, God is passionate about purity and fidelity before and after marriage. He only has your best in mind. He has heard all the prayers of regrets and the teary confessions. He's been in on all the marriage counseling sessions that dealt with the pain and difficulties caused by extramarital relationships. He wants to spare you all that, and He wants to bless you beyond what you can imagine. So He insists that you make purity an absolute priority in your life.

In lifelong commitment to a member of the opposite sex, there is deep pleasure in becoming saturated with the glue of romantic love and physical affection and binding yourself to a spouse who also is saturated with this God-given glue. There is joy in fidelity – in knowing that your wife is the only woman you will ever bond to and that you, in return, can have all of her because you are the only guy she has or ever will bond to. The idealization that comes with infatuation becomes a great blessing in marriage. When Heidi is under the spell of romantic love and passion is strong, in that moment I am the most wonderful guy in the world, my looks are flawless, and I have wit and charm beyond what mere mortals can comprehend. In this context, it is wonderful to be consumed by the fires of romance and I want no part in breaking the spell.

COMMITMENT BEFORE ROMANCE

Because of the permanence of the glue and the power of the flames, I believe that true purity calls for saving all romance and physical affection until both parties have committed to lifelong fidelity. In other words, you choose to not light a fire until there is a fireplace strong enough to contain it. You choose to not spend a lot of time gluing yourself to someone you're not sure you want to stick to permanently. I believe there is much wisdom and protection in keeping your pre-commitment relationships with members of the opposite sex at a non-romantic level. That means refraining from telling them that you love them in that "you and only you" way, refraining from romantic affection (kissing, hand-holding, slow dancing, etc.) and from too much time alone together and intimate heart-to-heart talks.

One of the most common relationship flaws among singles is one person taking the relationship more seriously than the other person does. They will both say they are "committed" but this means different things to each one. The commitment I'm talking about is not simply saying, "For the time being, I love you and only you, but that could change someday." Rather, it's a choice to covenant before God to stay together for life and demonstrate that you're willing to live out your choice by becoming engaged and asking the body of Christ to hold you accountable to your commitment.

I think it is very important that this commitment level be spelled out clearly and have actions that back it up. When a couple is in love, of course they feel committed – that's the nature of love. But it is necessary to ask yourself and your lover if this commitment is a mere feeling or a choice you are both willing to stand behind. If your boyfriend says he is "committed" but is not ready to commit to marriage, his commitment is not strong enough to warrant giving your heart or body to him. If he was truly committed, he would jump at the opportunity to prove it by committing to marriage.

I know this idea may sound strange and maybe even impossible to implement, but my wife and I and many other young couples we know have used the commitment before romance principle in our relationships and have greatly enjoyed the results. Now I need to be clear: I am not saying that there needs to be commitment before you get into any kind of relationship with the opposite sex. It is fine and important to have fun with them and to develop quality relationships. There are all kinds of enjoyable, non-romantic activities you can do together that will enable you to develop close friendships. Young people need healthy relationships that allow them to get to know each other as friends before they have all the pressure of being lovers. However, young people need to make sure that they are willing to stay together for life before they start enjoying the things that are designed to cement two souls together.

I'm also not saying that you should commit early in the relationship. It is crucial that you know a person very well before you commit to him or her. But you can get to know a person well enough to commit without first enjoying romance together. Like I mentioned before, romantic activities can blind your eyes from seeing what a person really is like. Physical touch is powerful and can make you feel like the person you are with is more wonderful than he or she really is. Infatuation is a breathtaking ride down a very slippery slide. Once you start, it is very hard to stop. Before you dive into romance, take every precaution necessary to make sure this is someone you are willing to be tied to for the long haul.

In His Word, God is clear that He delights in bringing young people together into a wonderful lifelong affair. He also loves us as a good father does his children. And as a Father, He longs to protect us from the painful consequences that come from misusing this gift.

When a man and woman begin giving their hearts, minds, eyes, and bodies to each other, God wants to bless them. He designed the whole process. He wants to see it enjoyed to the fullest! But we can't change the fact that love is meant to be lifelong. Before a couple begins bonding their hearts together, they should know for sure that this is the person that they want to commit to for the rest of their life and that they are mature enough to handle the responsibilities of sharing a family.

You said we should keep all romance till after a marriage commitment. Are you saying we shouldn't even hold hands or have intimate conversations until the wedding day?

What I'm suggesting is that all romance, i.e. the things that cause soul ties, including love notes, hand holding, long intimate conversations, etc, should be saved till engagement or an unbreakable commitment to marriage, but the sexual aspects of the relationship should be saved till the wedding day. I think the Hebrew pattern of betrothal is helpful here. When a couple was betrothed, a divorce was required to break it off, even though they still were to keep sex until after the wedding day.

After engagement but before marriage, Heidi and I held hands and I put my arm around her. However, before we had taken our relationship to the level of romantic involvement, I made sure we were committed for life. Even though we weren't married until March 25, 2006, I viewed our commitment as an unbreakable one from the day I asked her to marry me. If some problem came up, I knew we would have to stick it out and deal with it; in the same way, if a problem arose in the first year of marriage, we would work through it. Divorce was not an option for either of us.

I've read a number of books that advise young people to feel free to break off the engagement at any time up until the wedding day. I agree that breaking off a relationship before it is physically consummated will have fewer consequences than one that is broken off after the honeymoon. I don't think breaking an engagement is as devastating as a divorce. However, engagement is a promise and God takes breaking promises very seriously. So if there is still in the back of the mind a possibility of a breakup, then it is wise for the couple to refrain from all romantic activities. I firmly believe that if a man is going to start taking the affections of a woman, he had better be prepared to stand by her come hell or high water! If there is any lingering doubt, he needs to protect both of them and keep emotional and physical distance.

I think that engagement gives the couple a secure time to begin bonding emotionally and spiritually in a way that will make the transition to married life much easier. Engagement is a time to get comfortable with each other without the pressures of living in the same house. Early on in our relationship, Heidi needed space to adjust to the idea of a wild, passionate, Syrian lover. But by the time we got married and started living with each other, we both felt very comfortable with each other.

While engagement is a time for a couple to bond emotionally and spiritually, God states very clearly that sex should be saved for after the wedding day, when the couple has covenanted before God and the church to stay together for life. Hebrews 13:4 states "Marriage is honorable among all, and the bed undefiled; but fornicators and adulterers God will judge." Sex inside the safety of marriage is praised all throughout Scripture, but any sexual act outside of marriage is deemed sexual immorality. God has His reasons for being so jealous to guard this sacred gift. The physical, mental, and emotional effects of having sex are irreversible. You have become one with the person you shared that act with (1 Corinthians 6:16). To tear away from someone after sexual bonding brings devastating damage. Marriage is a vow before God, the government, and the church to stay together for life. It is an institution of God designed to keep a man and a woman bound together for life. God hates divorce (Malachi 2:16) He hates to see the protective bonds broken.

The long term commitment of marriage alone provides a safe place to enjoy sex without the fear of future separation. Some couples feel that engagement or living together is marriage and that they don't need to have a piece of paper of a wedding ceremony to be married. But if this couple is truly committed, why wouldn't they want to make that public declaration? Is it because they are not ready for the permanence of real marriage? I wonder if these same couples, after they have broken up, now consider themselves divorced. Engagement or a promise to get married someday is not marriage, and sex outside of marriage, no matter how right it seems or good it feels in the moment, will bring consequences.

As to the question of what physical affection is acceptable during engagement, I don't think there are specific, universal laws regarding what kinds of affection engaged couples should or shouldn't express to each other before marriage. However, there are the clear principles I mentioned earlier: that men and women should not defraud each other sexually and that they are bound by the law of love to protect each other and put the needs of the other before their own. How these universal principles apply to couples will look different in each case.

Because sexual arousal was designed to end in intercourse, anything that causes arousal should be avoided because it will be an act of defrauding – stirring up a desire that can't be fulfilled. It is not loving or an act of deference to generate frustration in your partner. But what causes arousal will be different for each couple, not to mention each individual. For some couples, holding hands might produce too much arousal in one of the partners and should be avoided. Other couples might even be able to kiss and not get aroused, although I think that such a couple would be the exception. Most couples probably have too much passion to handle kissing without getting their motors running. It's easy to fall into a selfish mindset, thinking only of what you can handle and what an activity is doing to you. However, what gets a woman aroused is often different from what gets a man aroused. Each one needs to be sensitive to the effect a certain type of affection is having on the other and show deference.

Any kind of physical affection that would bring guilt into the relationship should be avoided at all costs. It simply isn't worth it! You will belong to each other for the rest of your life and after the wedding day, you can begin to enjoy all of each other guilt-free. You will never regret saving something for marriage, but you'll regret going too far before marriage.

When Heidi and I were engaged, our two priorities were to make it to the wedding day free of guilt and to demonstrate our trustworthiness to each other. I saw this time as a chance to show Heidi that I could be trusted to stick to our boundaries. We made a distinction between affection that got us aroused and affection that simply communicated love and protection. If anything started getting our motors running (it was different things for each of us), then we talked openly together about it and backed off. I am very happy to say that we made it to marriage and fulfilled our goals, and we thoroughly enjoyed kisses one to one thousand on our wedding day.

Heidi: While engaged, we called off-limit touch "not now" pleasures, instead of "not good" pleasures. That little distinction helped us to remember that the physical love we desired so much was truly a good thing given by a good God, and it also turned our focus to Him in times when we were filled with longing for each other.

I can't express well enough how much it meant to me to see Jesse demonstrate that he could be trusted. He didn't step outside our self-made boundaries, and when I told him about touch that got me going, he totally backed off. My respect for him grew and strengthened, because of the trustworthiness he showed me in upholding the decisions we'd made on touch.

WHAT IF I'VE ALREADY MESSED UP?

Jesse: Violating God's design for love, romance, and sex will bring pain and damage. You can't do things that destroy the engine of a sports car and expect it to run as smoothly as the vehicle that's well cared for. In fact, some kinds of damage will prevent a car from being able to run at all. Willful rejection of God's rules will do serious injury to your love life and pain is inevitable, not only to you but to others that your wrong choices will affect.

But here is the great news. It's never too late to start applying God's principles to your love life. God is both willing and able to bring healing to the wounds formed by your wrong choices. If you feel you have messed up, or if you have been the victim of painful relationships, please keep reading.

This is the exciting thing about Christianity: Though our wrong choices will have lifelong consequences, Jesus came to take what we ruined and restore it so that it is more pristine than it was in its original condition.

If you give your torn or callused heart over to Jesus, He can restore it, giving back to you a brand new heart. You can have another chance. In fact, giving your whole heart to your spouse is not something that just happens on your wedding day; it is a choice you make every day, and one that you can only make by God's grace.

If you have violated your purity, looked at immoral images, or given away part of your body, there is a second chance. You can repent and surrender yourself to Christ's lordship and let Him make all things new! You'll be given a clean slate because of what Jesus did on Calvary. You can have secondary virginity. Only through this purifying process can you be happily married. But if you want to be restored, you have to surrender your life to Him and seek to follow His will for your life. If you go on ignoring His design for romance, you'll continue to bring harm to yourself and many others. But when you bring your brokenness to God and submit to His plan, God can create unimaginable beauty into your life.

Saving yourself for your future spouse is not enough to ensure a successful marriage. If this were the case, a nun and a monk could step out of convent and monastery, marry, and stay blissfully married the rest of their lives. But in reality, they would still face struggles. Purity and fidelity are daily choices, not mere one-time commitments. Heidi and I are so grateful that we've been spared the consequences of multiple breakups, and that we entered marriage with a sticky piece of tape; our transition to married life has been so much smoother because of it. It has been much easier to learn to trust each other. We don't face the difficulties of feeling compared to past lovers, or struggle with the guilt and regret of past memories.

However, we are still such sinful people. Only when we humble ourselves and cry out to God for His grace, and cast ourselves on Him, do we find the divine grace we need to love each other selflessly. When we rely on God, our marriage is truly better than anything we could have imagined. But when we lose sight of God, our selfishness rises to the top and we begin to ruin a good thing. But God is always there, chipping away at our pride and selfishness, and when we repent before Him and each other, once again there is a sweet freshness to our relationship.

ROMANCE TO THE GLORY OF GOD
Some of you will write off our ideas as unattainable. But before you categorize me as a pie-in-the-sky idealist, remember that, by God's grace, I've worked through the trials of saving myself for my wife. I know what it's like to want a relationship and to have to say no to what my hormones are telling me. I know what it's like to be scorned for not having a

girlfriend. I know, however long or short the wait, that it's a difficult one. However, I have now also experienced the euphoria of knowing that I am the only guy who has ever held my wife's hand, that I'm the only guy who's kissed her lips, and that I belong completely to her and she belongs completely to me. Thankfully, I don't know the pain of bonding to a person only to have to tear my heart away, and for this I can only thank my merciful Creator, and encourage other young people to "do love" God's way and enjoy the results.

Yes, we agree that it is hard to save all romantic relationships till you have committed to marriage. It's tough to wait patiently for your future spouse. But it's not as painful as one breakup after another. You might say that you'll take the risk, though, because a pre-marriage romance is just too much fun to pass up, or it takes away some of your loneliness. However, you must ask yourself what motivation lies behind your current romance. Is it just for self-gratification? As followers of Christ, shouldn't we do things out of a higher motivation, namely, to glorify God? (1 Corinthians 10:31)

We need to ask ourselves if Christ is Lord of our love life. If He is not, we are subjecting ourselves to the lies of the one who seeks to kill, maim, and destroy. Satan wants to ruin your love life. The master of illusion and deception, he will make lust and harmful relationships look so enticing and harmless, but behind the shiny lure is a razor sharp fish hook, designed to keep you captive.

In contrast, if you surrender the control of your life to Jesus, making Him the Master of your romance, you will find that He only wants to bless you with satisfying, good things. You'll also find that Jesus has higher priorities for your life than romance. Don't get me wrong – romance is His idea! He gave you those desires, and He can fulfill them better than anyone else. But more important to God is the health of your soul and your relationship with Him. These ultimately matter far more, so don't be surprised if romance doesn't come along when you expect it. When it does come, I hope your relationship will still have the overarching purpose of making you Christ-like and advancing His kingdom.

God has demonstrated repeatedly that, with His unlimited power and wisdom, He is so trustworthy. He may bring you through difficulties, and you may experience disappointment along the way. But it's all part of His plan. Put yourself in the hands of a first-rate Author who knows how to write the ultimate "happy ending" story.

CHAPTER 3

RECOGNIZE THE REALITY OF YOUR
FUTURE SPOUSE

When I was single, I remember how the song, "Wait for Me" by Rebecca St. James, motivated me to continue saving my eyes, body and heart completely for my future wife. I rediscovered that song a year after Heidi and I were married and listened to it again. All those old feelings came back... remembering what it was like to long for lifetime companionship and wondering who I was going to marry. Tears came to my eyes when I realized that Heidi was The Girl, unknown to me for so many years, who'd been singing, "Wait for me!" God has blessed me more than I could ever have imagined in the wife department, and I'm so glad that I waited.

Think about it. Right now – if God has marriage in your future – your spouse is alive and waiting for you. He or she is a real person and the choices you make now will affect him or her just as much as the choices you make after you are married. It will be much easier to remain faithful to your future spouse after marriage if you are faithful to her or him before you are married. Begin being faithful even before you meet your spouse.

Recognizing that my future spouse was alive helped me so much during my single years. It gave me a place to channel all my affection and sexual energy. These longings for love and marriage are God-given and can't be destroyed. So rather than unsuccessfully trying to kill these desires, you can learn to direct them toward your future life companion. Fall in love as you write love notes and pray for him or her. Pray that he will stay strong and learn to be a godly leader. Pray that God will protect your future wife from physical and emotional harm.

Save your heart and your eyes for your future spouse. When you are tempted to look at something immoral, picture how your future wife would feel watching you give into the temptation. Or how would she feel seeing you flirt with or be affectionate toward another girl? Imagine how wonderful it will be to tell your wife that you are giving your eyes completely to her and focus on the joy there will be in knowing that she trusts you completely because you have been faithful for many years.

I need to add a word of caution. Some young people are so madly in love that they feel their relationship will last forever. But because they expect to eventually marry the person they are dating, they give away much of their purity and physical affection to their boyfriend or girlfriend. Then as they mature or change, they move apart and their hearts become scarred and broken after the breakup. I know of so many men and women who regret the physical interaction they got into because they rationalized that they were doing it with the person they would marry.

Don't be deceived! One of Satan's common ploys is to lull you into a false sense of security so that you give away what should belong only to your spouse. If you fall for this ploy, you will regret it later, and experience pain for years to come.

Again, God's rules are for your pleasure and to protect you from pain. Don't let a young man or woman take advantage of you until they have shown the commitment to back it up. Guys, until you put a wedding band on her finger, protect her like you want other men to be protecting your future wife. Don't lie to yourself by thinking, "She'll probably be my wife in the future, so I might as well enjoy her as a wife now!" For your own safety and hers, you need to see her as belonging to another man until you are willing to lay down your life for hers and abandon all others "till death do you part." If you are showing physical affection to a girl you have not committed to marrying, it's likely that you are having an affair with another man's wife and are stealing from him.

How far is it okay to go physically with a boyfriend or girl-friend?

I can't give you a hard line, but look at it this way. How far would you want a guy to go with your future wife? How far do you want your future husband to go with someone other than you? Picture your future wife on a date with some guy right now, as you are reading this. Do you feel comfortable with them kissing passionately? How about seeing them snuggled up on a couch? I know if I think about some guy doing these "innocent" things with Heidi, I get angry! I am passionate about my wife and so glad that she saved herself completely for me.

Girls, how do you feel about your future husband fondling another woman right now? Or seeing him cuddle with her in a car? If you are tempted to dress immodestly, think about how you would feel if you saw your husband ogling another woman in the outfit you're thinking about wearing. Think of the pleasure and gratitude your future husband will have, knowing that you kept your beauty and body only for him. But he's going to feel slighted if you're flaunting your precious treasure of beauty to any and every guy. What makes him more privileged than these other guys?

And if you're tempted to receive affection from a man you are not committed to, picture how your future husband would feel if he saw this.

Romantic affection differs from other forms of interaction because romance forms spiritual, emotional, and physical ties with members of the opposite gender. In romance there is a sense that you are being tied together, that you are becoming one. It is a delicious feeling. But those ties are real and meant to last forever. If you break apart from your special person, the ties between you continue to be real and will haunt you. During your single years, you should do everything you can to avoid such soul ties until you and your future spouse have thought things through, decided that you two could be in this forever, and then committed to each other for life.

Right up until marriage you need to guard each other's purity and keep the relationship guilt-free. You may think you are in a beautiful relationship with someone, and that you want to begin celebrating it with physical affection. If you are outside of marriage, I promise you that sexual physical affection will bring guilt into your relationship, if not right away, then for sure later on!

Guilt is a terrible poison to love and intimacy, because it drives you away from the openness and honesty that intimacy requires. You feel shame and want to hide. Guilt will spoil your relationship. So many people who engage in premarital sex often see their relationship end shortly after, because the burden of their guilt divides them.

I am not here to be prudish or legalistic about this; I'm simply asking you to look at a perspective you may not have thought much about. Right now your future spouse is alive and breathing! If you want the goons to keep their hands and lips off your future wife, it's only fair to return the favor and keep your own hands off someone else's future wife.

I emphasize this again, guys and girls: Don't fall into the trap of justifying your actions by thinking that the person you're flirting with or being physical with might be your future spouse. When you attach a real person to the thoughts that are reserved for your future spouse, you enter hazardous territory. You will be tempted to let your mind go places it shouldn't because you start believing this might be your future spouse. I know the trap. I would stir up my desires for love and marriage and tell myself I was falling in love with my future spouse. But then when my heart was hungry, I'd look for someone real to attach these feelings to. In most cases the best way to direct your affection to your real future spouse is to completely surrender your feelings and desires to God.

I have had a crush on several guys, but have not been in a real romantic relationship. Have I given part of my heart away?

I don't think so. Heidi liked several guys before she met me. In fact, she had some crushes that lasted years, but because she never communicated her interests to any of these guys and never acted on her feelings, she never gave her heart away. Heidi has communicated to me many times that I have her whole heart. (**Heidi:** You've got that right!)

I also liked several girls, but again, because I never entered a serious relationship, never gave physical affection, never wrote love notes, etc., I never developed any "soul ties" with anyone. Even though it was painful to be turned down by the two fathers that I mentioned earlier, it was not nearly as painful as I'd imagine a breakup would be. There is great safety in approaching the girl's father before beginning a relationship. I was so grateful I had taken that first step that served to protect both my heart and the girls' hearts.

Giving your whole heart to your spouse is not a one-time thing, but a daily decision. Hearts wander. Marriage is daily commitment to your spouse that says, "I love you and only you and I love you with my whole heart." When you cannot say that truthfully, you need to get on your knees, repent, and work at making it a true statement.

If you've struggled with infatuation or crushes and feel bad about having given part of your heart away, I want to encourage you that you haven't. This is not to say that unchecked infatuation is harmless. It's not. Proverbs 4:23 warns, "Keep your heart with all diligence, for out of it spring the issues of life." Secret crushes are weeds that can grow out of control, choking your spiritual life. If you act on these feelings, you may find yourself in a dangerous position. I have seen many young people run away from home and abandon their faith because they were involved in a wrong relationship that consumed them.

Infatuation is a powerful force that, if left unchecked, will cast a spell on you that distorts your sense of right and wrong. You may feel like your attraction is so strong that you are helpless against it. Don't believe it. You always have the choice to submit your desires to God and give Him control of your love life. Romantic passion is a consuming fire that often starts with little unchecked fantasies. Be on guard! These "harmless" daydreams are little termites that eat away at your foundations if you let them. On the outside, you'll appear as strong as ever, but inside you're growing weaker and more susceptible to falling. Like the Casting Crowns song, "Slow Fade," warns, "People never crumble in a day. It's a slow fade when you give your heart away."

I want you to be cautious and mindful of the danger, but I don't want you to feel burdened by guilt. Attractions are a normal and healthy part of growing up. Share them with your parents; verbalizing your attractions and getting your parents' input will both help you see things in a more realistic light. Let your crushes inspire you to prepare for the day when you are ready for marriage, but most importantly, surrender them to God and let Him bring things to pass in His perfect time. "Delight yourself in the Lord and He will give you the desires of your heart." (Psalm 37:4).

I was most content as a single when my heart was asleep. God doesn't want the single years to be consumed by a lot of desires that can't be fulfilled. As a single, you have a tremendous opportunity to serve God with an intense, undistracted focus. Make the most of this time and play the roles given you to the best of your abilities.

You'll face temptation and pressures to compromise and sometimes the enemy's poison will look so appealing. You need a vision that inspires you, that will give you the strength to stay strong and committed. Guys, think about how wonderful it will be to stand before your future wife, tall and strong, knowing that you have fought the good fight and have a whole, unblemished heart and unsullied mind to offer your wife. Girls, think about how much joy you will be able to give your husband when you present yourself to him for the first time. Do you have any idea how much it will thrill him to know that he's the only guy you've given yourself to?

If such a thought fills you with regret because of what you have already lost, I want to remind you that an even greater gift than an unblemished heart is a heart that is fully surrendered to God, and the purity that comes from being cleansed by Christ's blood is richer, and deeper than any man-made attempts at purity. Christ can make you whiter than snow and completely clean your slate. Your union with your future spouse can be filled with delight, but between now and then, you both will face obstacles and challenges designed to rob you of this delight. Your future spouse is worth all the challenges you will face. Let your imagination soar as you anticipate how wonderful it will be to enter marriage pure and whole. Let that vision be your strength.

CHAPTER 4

THE TRUTH ABOUT SOUL-MATES, SEXUAL COMPATIBILITY, AND FINDING "THE ONE"

Our culture has a lot of false assumptions about what it takes to make a great marriage, such as the idea that true love is something you discover or magically fall into – the result of two people finding their "soul mate" or "other half." In reality, true love is the result of hard work, selfless devotion, and a reliance on God. What I said earlier about how you can find the right spouse without experimenting romantically probably raised a lot of questions. Maybe you disagree. That's okay. In this chapter I want to come at the topic from a couple of different angles and take the time to answer some questions or objections you may have so far on this issue.

If we don't enjoy a romantic relationship, how will I know if this person is my soul mate or if we have good chemistry?

Even in Christian circles, there is the false notion that somewhere out there is your other half – someone who will immediately understand your every thought and mood swing, whose kiss will set off never-ending fireworks. I've seen movies where two characters will kiss to see if there is chemistry between them. When the sparks don't fly like they should, the couple assumes that they are not right for each other. I'm glad I didn't use that ridiculous evaluation step when I decided on Heidi. Our first kiss was on our wedding day; I'd had no training in kissing. I didn't know you weren't supposed to lick your lips, which I did, and almost slid right off her mouth. Did this mean we didn't have chemistry or weren't soul mates? No, it meant I didn't know how to kiss. Once I learned… (**Heidi and Jesse:** Wow!)

Married people who have these wrong ideas about chemistry and soul mates find themselves in a predicament when they meet someone that they are strongly attracted to. They conclude that they must have married the wrong person and now they've found the real soul mate they should have married. What do they do? Sadly, some opt for divorce and remarriage, only to discover that infatuation can be a teller of lies.

The truth is that the only real "soul mate" arises from years of working to build a relationship with your spouse, sharing life's struggles together, learning to communicate and to speak each other's love language.

Sure, you will meet someone you are strongly attracted to. Your eyes will lock in an incomparably heart-melting moment of connection. Don't be fooled. Sexual attraction let loose can be indiscriminate, needing only a pretty body or face. It doesn't care about the deeper things like selflessness and commitment. If you "follow your heart" (code for "follow your sex drive") you will meet ruin. The only way your sex drive can be satisfied is by bringing it under the lordship of Christ and training yourself to be satisfied in the context of marriage. The chemistry found in infatuation can be a counterfeit, temporary thing, no matter how strong and real its pull on you. Truly satisfying love is found in loving the one you marry, not simply marrying the one you love.

Earlier I pointed out that the feelings of love are like a fire. In marriage, the fire can go out. But you can rekindle the blaze with physical affection, flirting, special gifts, love notes, words of affirmation, etc. Once you have in place the commitment to stay together, make a choice to keep the fires going and you will never doubt the chemistry between you.

How can we know if we are sexually compatible if we don't do some experimenting?

Sexual compatibility is not simply a matter of two people finding someone else with the right genetic make-up. Sexual attraction is a very complex issue. For whatever reason, some people will be more sexually attractive to you than others. People will argue that you should marry someone who really turns you on sexually. I agree that there should be lots of spark and attraction in marriage, but I disagree that we need to find our certain "type" to be sexually fulfilled. Learning how to be satisfied sexually and how to satisfy your spouse is an art that has to be learned. Movies and novels will sell you the idea that all you have to do is put two sexually compatible people together and their experience will be wonderful. It is easy to create that perfect scenario in fantasy, but in real life there are so many more issues that have to be worked through.

When you enter the safe framework of marriage, there are some delightful and awkward lessons and techniques in physical intimacy for you to learn. It isn't something you can prepare for because each person is unique and you will have to discover your spouse's individual formula for what pleasures them. To ensure sexual compatibility, you need to understand the immaterial side of sex – soul intimacy.

SEX AND SOUL INTIMACY

Our desire for sexual intimacy has two sides to it. There is the physical side, which is fueled by desires for physical release and nerve stimulation. In this physical aspect of sex, it's possible to create pleasurable ecstasy outside of marriage and there are all kinds of immoral ways to find sexual enjoyment. I don't speak from experience, but I'm sure, before the consequences, that there are a lot of pleasurable sensations in wild, unfettered sex. Yet God designed sex to be much more than physical release or nerve pleasure. There is an immaterial aspect to sex, as well – two souls who are becoming one with each other. Beyond the physical, we also long for spiritual and emotional intimacy. Most kids figure out what has to happen for physical intimacy to take place, but many adults never figure out how to have soul intimacy. Soul intimacy is developed as two people discover the satisfaction of knowing each other fully – their deepest dreams, hurts, passions, and weaknesses. It is found in shared experiences of joy and pain and a willingness to reveal who you really are.

The physical is supposed to be a celebration of the emotional and spiritual intimacy that is being forged between a man and woman. When sex is reduced to a selfish pursuit of physical sensations, it becomes a consuming force that will actually prevent you from being able to find soul intimacy. In contrast, when soul intimacy is formed, the physical side will be full of variety, excitement, and comfort. To forge soul intimacy requires three basic components: trust, fidelity, and selflessness. If these are in place, you'll never have to worry about sexual compatibility. However, if even one of these elements is missing, it will throw a big damper on the fires of passion and cause real trouble in the bedroom.

Trust

Soul intimacy requires exposing the most vulnerable areas of who you are, revealing painful and embarrassing secrets about your past, putting down your weapons, and taking off your armor. Of course, doing this requires great trust that the other person will not take advantage of your defenseless state. If your spouse doesn't trust you, they will keep their armor on to conceal parts of themselves. Gaining a person's trust requires great tenderness and absolute commitment to their safety. Anger or harsh words will drive couples apart. A track record of previous romantic entanglements will also make trust more difficult to build.

Fidelity

In marital intimacy, there is only room for two. Nothing short-circuits intimacy like betrayal. Infidelity of any kind, mental or physical, straying eyes, or straying hands, will bring real guilt into the equation. Guilt destroys intimacy. Intimacy requires disclosure, while guilt makes you want to run from it. There are a host of problems that are the result of participating in illicit sexual pleasure. We feel so strongly about the need for sexual purity that we have included a whole chapter on defeating lust and reclaiming purity. If you want real intimacy, pursue purity with a passion.

SELFLESSNESS

One of God's purposes for sex is to bring us out of the trap of self-centeredness and experience the joy of having our eyes turned toward someone else. Sexual ecstasy comes as an act of total surrender to the other person. But when sex becomes a selfish pursuit it will make you feel empty. Many couples say that their sex life is most fulfilling when both spouses' goal is to serve and pleasure the other. If either person is critically evaluating how the other is meeting their sexual needs, they'll be disappointed.

THE SEXUAL REALITY

It's easy for a single person to fall into the trap of thinking that marriage is all about sex, and sometimes desires for marriage are simply desires for sex. Our sexual desires are a huge part of who God made us to be. But many people make the mistake of marrying someone based on sexual attraction alone. In reality, marriage is two people experiencing life together and sex plays a much smaller role in that shared life than most singles imagine. If things are going great, the sexual aspect of marriage will use up maybe one hour out of every forty-eight. So if your relationship is going to be successful, it had better be based on something else for the other ninety-seven percent of the time.

I'm not trying to demean the beauty or importance of sex, but I want to emphasize that for marriage to work, it has to be based on friendship and character. You need your wife or husband to be a great friend, not just a great lover. And it's inner beauty that makes for great friendships. When making the decision of a life partner, you need to ask, "If I removed the sexual aspect, would I still enjoy this person as a friend?" There are people who know how to play sexual games and turn you on, but they have little depth of character. Sexual desire alone cannot sustain a marriage; there must be deep friendship and selfless commitment.

Sexual tastes and what turns you on can be trained and cultivated within the empowering confines of marriage. But if you let yourself be controlled by your appetites they can and will destroy you.

Won't sex in marriage with only one person get boring? I thought variety was the spice of life?

J. Budziszewski says that there are two kinds of variety: superficial variety and deep variety. The superficial kind is found in having casual sex with lots of different women. It is like wading ankle deep in fifteen different kiddie pools. He says there is also deep variety which is found in exploring the depths of one woman, which is like swimming in the ocean. It is truly amazing to keep getting deeper and deeper into my relationship with Heidi. There is still much of her that is a mystery to me, but I'm thrilled that I have the rest of my life to keep exploring her.

Commitment to one woman allows for a deeper more satisfying type of variety. Budziszewski goes on to address the man who wants the depths of intimacy, but doesn't want the bondage of long-term commitment.

"Is this your thought? If so, you may as well forget it. Outside of marriage there's not a chance for that kind of intimacy.... Why is that? The reason is a great secret, although it shouldn't be.

You want to keep your options open, but intimacy requires throwing them away.

Did you hear that? Let me say it again. You want to keep your options open, but intimacy requires throwing them away. That's why lovers have to be married, and that's why marriage has to be permanent. If you and your girlfriend haven't given your lives to each other for good, you'll always be holding back from each other, whether you know it or not. In fact, you'd be crazy not to. Why should you open all your treasures to someone who might leave you? Why should she? But "holding back" is another way of saying you're not swimming in the ocean after all. You may reach for her depths, but you'll only bruise your heart on the wading pool floor. You may think you're swimming in the ocean because you can't feel the bottom. But that's only because you're not reaching for it, and neither is she."

How can I know that I am willing to commit to someone if I don't have a romantic relationship with him/her first? In a commitment-first relationship, isn't there a danger of rushing into something you may regret later?

For whatever reason, some people have the idea that it's okay to enter a romantic relationship lightly as long as you don't enter marriage lightly. Consequently, there are lots of Christian guys who are fearful of commitment, but have no problem taking advantage of women by leading them on and enjoying the benefits of romance. It is dangerous to enjoy romance outside of a marriage commitment (Proverbs 6:20-35). Commitment first can prevent so much heartache!

Remember, I'm not saying you should rush into commitment in just any relationship. This decision is huge – one of the biggest you will ever make. Bathe it in prayer, seek counsel, and ask questions of those who know the other person better. You need to know for sure that you're making a wise move. Before you commit to marriage, you need to know this person. However, a romantic relationship of infatuation is the worst time to evaluate someone as a potential marriage partner. Love is blind and hormones are not a good judge of character. I know the excitement of sitting close to a special someone, of physical affection, and how a romantic note can sweep you off your feet. It isn't wise to make the critical choice of life partner under such circumstances. Many people have mistaken lust and physical excitement for true love and jumped into marriage. But it takes a lot more than physical attraction to keep two people together.

We're cautioning you that any romantic involvement is a serious thing – you are binding yourself to someone with superglue that has been designed to last for life. We suggest that, prior to commitment, all relationships should be kept to a level of what would be acceptable for a married man to do with a woman who is not his wife. Don't start gluing yourself to someone you're not ready to commit to.

To clarify, let's say you are a single girl, hungry for marriage. Along comes a dashing young man who wants to start a relationship with you. From the little you've observed, he has some great qualities, but you would like to get to know him better. I'm not at all suggesting that you tell this guy that unless he is ready to propose and set the date, you want nothing to do with him. How to scare a guy away! If that is your mode of operation, you may be single a long time! However, your mindset needs to be that unless this guy really, truly commits to you, then in all likelihood, your future husband is still out there and you need to stay faithful to him. Be careful not to give away anything that belongs to him or to do something that will bring harm to your future marriage. In your mind, bring your future husband along as a chaperone (but maybe don't talk to him, though). Evaluate how he would feel about your activities. Again, this is not a rule you have to follow, but a practical suggestion meant to spare you pain.

In the above scenario, it's important to be upfront that you aren't interested in a casual fling. Tactfully let that dashing young man know that while you would enjoy getting to know him, you will be on guard to save certain things for the man who is willing to commit for life. If this fellow is worthy of you, such a statement will make you very attractive in his eyes!

He will see right away what a treasure you are. But if your words scare him away, be thankful – he isn't worth the pain!

You may want to start a relationship with someone to just experiment and get to know each other to see if there is something between you. But be careful. Before you know it, you may have moved right past the evaluating stage to making out, skipping over the important question, "Is this the person I'm willing to spend the rest of my life with?" A single man and a single woman are powder kegs of emotions and hormones. A casual platonic "get to know you" relationship in theory sounds like a wonderful idea. In the real world, though, this idea is like lighting a torch in a dark basement to see if fireworks are stored down there. You need to recognize the danger and take the necessary precautions.

Just to make my point crystal clear, I must repeat: Before you commit to marriage, you need to know the other person. Make this critical decision objectively and prayerfully. Be alert and aware! Like Benjamin Franklin wisely suggested, "Men should keep their eyes wide open before marriage and half-shut afterward." To be objective, you need to keep physical and emotional distance while you make the decision so that you get to know the real person, not just the effect he or she has on your hormones. Then when you are confident that you are ready for marriage, and that you are willing to sacrifice your life for this person and cherish and protect him or her for the rest of your life, you can commit to marriage and begin enjoying God's wonderful gift.

What if I marry the wrong person?

God has given us clear guidelines about marriage. A believer is not to marry an unbeliever (2 Corinthians 6:14) and you are not to marry a person of the same gender (Mark 10:6-7; Romans 1:26-27). But if you have already married someone of the opposite gender, you can know with confidence that you are married to the "right" person. You may make a foolish decision about who you will marry, but you never marry the wrong person. Once you've said your wedding vows, you are married to the person God wants you to commit to for the rest of your life! No matter what life throws at you, He wants you to stick it out. God hates divorce (Malachi 2:16)! Asking if you missed the person God had for you or if you married someone you shouldn't have is a totally worthless question after the wedding day. Because you vowed to be faithful till death, this is the person God wants you to be with! Did God have someone better for you? I doubt it. God knew in advance the person you were going to marry, so I don't think He wasted time getting someone else ready for you and now that person is left high and dry!

I have been disappointed by the advice being given to young people today about how to find the right spouse. Several books counseled teens to become involved romantically with several different young people to see what they liked in the opposite gender. A single man in his late thirties wrote to warn young people that they could never be too careful about commitment and shared that he would back out of a relationship if he didn't like where things were going. At first blush, it may seem like good advice. But it contains a dangerous element: You're encouraged to be critical of the other person and to break things off when you encounter difficulties in the relationship. If you have let these principles guide your romantic relationships, when the time comes to marry someone and you want to be committed for life, your habits of criticism and breakups are going to be a real threat to your marriage. If you've trained yourself to break off relationships at the first sign of trouble, it'll be easy to convince yourself that the conflict you're facing is the other person's fault and in your own mind, you'll come off smelling like a rose.

In marriage, however, it is not an option to break up when you encounter difficulties. Instead you are forced to learn to work through your problems, which can only be resolved when both people ask themselves what they can do to patch things up. As long as both spouses are blaming each other, the conflict will go on indefinitely.

No matter how long you wait or how picky you are about finding a spouse, conflicts will happen. Even if you find the "perfect" person in your dating years, that person will change. It is a fact of life: people are always changing. We are being drawn by the Holy Spirit to be shaped into the image of Christ, but there are also many forces pulling us away from God. On top of that, our circumstances are constantly affecting us. Grief, weight gain, injury, illness, parenthood, or job change will influence the type of person we are becoming. Who we are is a very fluid concept. So if you're looking for the perfect spouse to make you happy, you will never find him or her. You need to wisely choose the person you marry, but ultimately true love is about sacrifice and giving. If you are waiting for the person who will meet all your needs, you might as well plan on being permanently single. Your true marital satisfaction only comes when your focus is, "How can I bless my spouse? How can I serve him? What can I do to make her happy?" Through the act of giving, we become truly satisfied.

I grieve when I hear Christians tell a "you can never be too cautious" story about some poor person who married the "wrong" person. In these stories, the problem is not that one person married the wrong person, but that one of them stopped being the right person. No matter who you marry, you will have difficulties. If you are selfless the whole first year, you rejoice that you have married the right person. But if after the first year you become selfish – say, because of stress at work – and you now have marriage problems, did you marry the wrong person? No, of course not: Finding the right person means working hard at remaining the right person.

But here is encouragement. God has given both men and women tremendous influence over their spouse. If you truly work at doing all you can in the relationship, you will be rewarded. I wasn't afraid to commit to Heidi because I knew that if I loved her like Christ loved us, if I fulfilled my duty to wash her with the Word, and truly laid down my rights for her, and if I was really focused on giving rather than getting, I would not be disappointed. If you work on being the right person, you most likely will be happily married, but if you constantly criticize your spouse and evaluate whether or not you married the right person, you will be very dissatisfied.

Are you saying I could marry any Christian and make it work?

Partly, yes. I think far too much is made of finding the "perfect one for you." We each have our ideas about what will make us "compatible". But it's easy to let this search for the "right one" become selfishly motivated. We want what is best for "me." It can become like a search for the perfect car or house: "What qualities do I need in a spouse to make me happy and fulfill my needs?" Like I said earlier, such questions won't work in marriage. Our job in marriage is to serve, protect, and cherish our spouse. You can do this for anyone because it is a choice that lies within you. In our culture, we have so much freedom in our choice of life partner, but our success rate in staying together is appallingly low!

In other cultures where marriages are arranged by parents or others, there is often more commitment and staying power, because the couples understand the truth of the maxim, "love the one you marry, rather than marry the one you love." Yes, of course there are many loveless marriages in places where the couples are not free to choose, and no, I am not suggesting arranged marriage as a rule. I am simply pointing out that any man and a woman, committed to the welfare and needs of the other, and empowered by God's love, can create beautiful love and romance.

A couple of months into our relationship, I started to doubt whether Heidi and I were "compatible." I'd been hurt by a petty misunderstanding, and grew critical. I doubted whether Heidi really loved me – whether she could communicate it in a way I would feel as love. I actually began to feel trapped and second-guessed my decision. But that same night I spilled my feelings and tears to Heidi and we got the issue resolved.

My focus had made the fatal switch from asking how I could love Heidi to evaluating how she was loving me. Since then there have been times we've disagreed on things and have failed to meet each other's expectations, but we have been realizing that truly loving your spouse is something that can be learned.

Does this mean you should go and marry the next cute Christian you see? No! Much prayer and seeking God for guidance should go into this decision. God will make things clear to you; He has the power to prevent a relationship that He does not want for you and can open the way for the one He does. Yes, it is your job to make your marriage work, but choices have consequences. You can make sinful choices that will rob your future marriage of freedom and pleasure. You can create burdens of guilt and habits that will make true romance very difficult. If you decide to marry someone who has made many of these wrong choices, know that he or she will bring baggage that will add challenges to your relationship. Does this mean that God would never want you to marry such a person? No, because marriage is about sacrificial love.

There are many times that He asks men and women to sacrifice personal comfort and ease to bring healing to others. For example, let's say that a woman spent many years living immorally and has been ravaged by sin. Now she has surrendered her life to Christ and wants to serve Him wholeheartedly. A young man feels that God is asking him to marry this woman, even though he knows she'll bring many painful problems into marriage. They'll have trouble building trust and finding real fulfillment in sex because of the guilt, fears, and insecurities that her past sins have caused. But because the man knows with confidence that this is God's will for him, he will take these burdens on himself and follow Christ's example of sacrificial love. As they learn to love and serve, God will create tremendous beauty from the ashes and can restore the wife to be a pure, beautiful woman of God who will bring deep joy to her husband.

The key thing to remember in choosing your life partner is that you should be getting married for God's purposes, not simply to meet your personal needs. Marriage is so much more than an outlet for sexual release or a place for you to find a satisfying intimate relationship. It is a tool that God will use to shape us and accomplish His goals for us. Your primary purpose in life is not finding the perfect spouse, but becoming the person God wants you to be and fulfilling your calling. If God does lead you to seek a marriage partner, make sure you look for a spouse who will aid and enable you to accomplish what God has called you to do.

What do you suggest in the case of a long distance attraction where the couple wants to start a relationship, but they don't know each other enough to commit to marriage?

Heidi and I are thankful that we lived only an hour and a half apart and saw each other fairly often, so we knew each other well enough to commit, but a lot of other couples don't find themselves in the same situation. In these cases, it's important that the couple get to know each other in a wholesome and pure way. For the safety of both involved, I think physical and emotional distance needs to be had. I believe it is possible to get to know someone very well before there is romantic involvement. Sterile questions and clinical investigation may not seem romantic or particularly comfortable, but there is a lot of wisdom getting to know each other in a safe but effective way. Find out from mutual friends or others who spend a lot of time with him/her whether this person exhibits the important qualities you want in a spouse. (See Chapter 5 for specifics you may want to ask regarding the other person.) If you're not comfortable sleuthing yourself, perhaps ask your parents, a mentor, or trustworthy friend to help you out.

I have a friend, Steve (name changed), who told me about an experience he had that illustrates my point. Shortly after high school, Steve asked a girl to go out with him. She declined and his interest in her subsequently declined. Years later, this girl contacted Steve and said she was now interested in him and was curious where his heart was. A little taken aback, Steve said he was no longer interested, but that he would be open to getting reacquainted. They did some fun stuff together, such as going golfing, but Steve was cautious about going ahead with things before he had some issues settled. He took her to dinner and started asking her some tough questions. Puzzled, the girl wanted to know, "Is this an interview?"

Steve later decided that she was not the one for him and didn't pursue any further exclusive time. He may not have come off as the most romantic flower in the vase, but he was able to get to the heart of the issue and realize this relationship would not work. I respect him for his wisdom in protecting this young woman by being clear and upfront.

I would suggest caution here though, because once an experimental relationship is started, and there is a possibility of marriage, it is going to be very exciting for someone who has years of pent-up emotions. There's a danger of easing into the romantic side of things before the couple has decided on commitment. Be careful that you don't find yourself emotionally and physically involved before you have made a final decision. It isn't enough to just take things slow, there needs to be a deliberate protection during this time; purity won't just happen.

If you are the young man in this position, you need to decide if you want to commit or if you need more confirmation. If you decide you don't know the woman well enough to commit, then it is your job to protect the young woman's heart and not take advantage of her while she is in an emotionally vulnerable state. God designed you to be the initiator and the protector. Once you start tampering with her affections and trying to win her heart, you have a God-given responsibility to commit and sacrifice your rights for her! (Ephesians 5:22-33; 1 Thessalonians 4:6) Give her both the freedom to break things off, and also the security of knowing that you are not going anywhere. But at the same time, until she commits to you in return, protect her physically and emotionally as if she belongs to another man. Continue to guard your heart and mind so that if this woman does decide you are not the one, you will not carry excess baggage into a relationship with another woman.

And to the young woman: Until he puts a ring on your finger, stay reserved and don't give away anything you will regret if this relationship falls through. Don't become desperate and do everything you can to keep him interested. Put your trust in God and allow him to work in the young man's heart. If he is so fickle that you feel you need to constantly woo him, he is not worthy of you. Conversely, during this time of getting to know each other and discovering if you two are right for each other, don't judge him for not being romantic. If he is holding back and trying to protect your heart, applaud him! Don't simply check to see if he makes you swoon – a lot of losers can make you do that – rather, check whether he has moral freedom, purpose in life, a dependent walk with God, and other things you deem are important.

I hope you don't feel that I'm writing all this because I think I know exactly how things should work in relationships or am convinced that you have to follow my formula. Hardly! I simply believe these are wise precautions that will prevent a lot of heartbreak. Relationships are often messy and they involve risk. There is no way to guarantee a foolproof, pain-free way to start a relationship. However, not all romantic pain is created equal. Disappointment is a much different kind of pain than a severed "soul tie." When I was turned down by those two fathers, I was filled with disappointment. I had many hopes and expectations that were crushed. But God used that pain to purify me, to teach me to trust Him, and to cleanse my heart from wrongful infatuation. Heidi went through similar disappointments. When we share these painful memories with each other, we are filled with compassion and love for each other.

However, I can only imagine – and others have told me this – that severed soul ties are a different story completely. Shared infatuation and romance will cause hearts to become woven together as they merge their identities, making memories together. Even imagining what this would be like is very painful for me. It makes me sick just picturing Heidi writing one of her fabulous love letters to another guy, and knowing that he forever has a part of her past locked away in his keeping. Thinking of her communicating her love physically to another guy is a thought I want no part of. She hasn't done this, but she did experience disappointment. Thankfully, neither of us has to struggle with these thoughts because God spared us this kind of pain. Trips down memory lane fill us with renewed wonder at the beauty of love.

I am not suggesting caution simply so you can avoid pain. Pain can be a wonderful thing that humbles and drives us to the Savior. That being said, I do believe that we should strive to glorify God in this area of romance and continue to seek His best. True love and romance can only be found in selfless love, not in looking for self-gratification but in seeking what is best for the one you love. Do everything you can to protect the one you are interested in. It is one thing to be reckless with your own heart, but you have a grave responsibility to protect the hearts of others. Let "do to others as you would have them do to you" be your guide.

Dating or courtship?

Dating has become a loaded, controversial term in many circles. I have read books on both sides of the debate. The majority of these books actually agree with each other on most points but often use the term "dating" in different ways. I don't want to join the controversy and argue for one side or the other. My wife and I are not proposing a sure-fire method that you have to follow. In fact, I think discussions about procedure can miss the more important elements in finding a godly spouse. The labels courtship, dating, and betrothal sometimes only muddy the water. I poked fun at these labels by telling people that Heidi and I were "arranged to begin courting, by dating, during our time of betrothal."

The specific steps you follow are not nearly as important to the health of your relationship as are the more foundational principles: keeping God at the center, laying aside your rights and demonstrating selfless love to your spouse, and working to become Mr. Right rather than working overtime to find Miss Right. My parents dated each other for several years before they committed to marriage and they have had one of the most successful marriages that I know of. There is no magic formula for finding a spouse – no set pattern. God is too creative for that. Every love story He writes is unique.

Let God write your love story instead of wandering around the School of Hard Knocks, hoping to bump into your wife- or husband-to-be.

What I am suggesting won't work if you leave God out of the picture. But when you factor in your loving, wise, all-powerful Creator, love becomes an exciting adventure. God designed love, sex, and romance. He created each man and woman unique. It follows then that God is the ultimate Matchmaker – better than any dating service. He knows you better than you know yourself. He knows not only what you really want in a spouse but also what you need.

GOD KNOWS BEST

I hope these answers have helped clarify our views. In conclusion, whether you date or court or even have an arranged marriage, how you come together is not nearly as important as daily reliance on God – finding His grace and forgiveness. Breaking God's design will always bring devastating consequences. There is healing for mistakes, yet there is also such great blessing in going God's way from the beginning. I pray that you will not listen to Satan's lies about love, sex, and romance. Save yourself for the one you will spend the rest of your life with. God knows best and He will reward you.

CHAPTER 5

KNOW WHAT YOU NEED IN A SPOUSE

Dear Future Husband,   June 1999

I believe I should know what I'm looking for in a husband – and I think fifteen is not too young to begin. I don't know you yet, but I know God has already decided you will be my husband.

To prepare you for the following, I want you to know that my list is aiming high, and although you can't ever measure up perfectly to my standards, my desire is that you come close.

1. You must be a born-again Christian with a sincere and fervent desire to love and follow God all your life. You must believe that only Christ's blood and forgiveness is what saves you from your sins and gives you entrance to heaven.

2. I desire a husband who loves children; I don't require it, but only ask if you'd be willing to adopt children other than our own. That is one dream close to my heart, which I pray will someday come true if it is in God's will.

3. I would like you to be responsible in everything, especially your work. You must be able to support us after we are married.

4. Since I am planning to spend the rest of my life with you, I hope I will like your looks. I.e. you'll have to be handsome. Oh, and you'll also have to have experience in the cooking, doing laundry, and housework realm.

5. You must be honest, dedicated, gentle, devoted, determined, level-headed, wise, and – you have to know how to laugh even during the hard times.

6. I want you to be able to accept and love my parents and siblings as if they were your own. And I will require the same of myself for your family. I also desire that your family will accept me wholeheartedly.

7. Along the same line, you must come from a family background whose foundation is Christ Jesus. Your parents must be Christians as well.

8. You must be able to interact well with all ages and all kinds of people. If that's too hard for you, I'll narrow it down to all ages.

That's as many requirements as I could think of for now. I know that there are a lot of them and may seem overwhelming, but that's because they're 'aiming high' standards.

Finally, I pray we will learn to love each other with the agape love Christ had; that we will stand by each other 'for better or for worse.'

I can't wait to meet you! I'm sure you're very special.

Your Future Wife,

Heidi Ruth

Heidi: I laughed pretty hard when I typed this letter into the book. Wow, talk about a strong-minded girl who lays down the requirements hard and fast! Well, I got my hot guy who knows his way around the kitchen and fulfilled # 4 to a tee, and I'm very, very happy with him!

I'm glad I aimed high for a spouse – Jesse was bang on – but I regret not having spent more time during those years seeking to gain similar high qualities in myself. Jesse was the one who didn't write up a list; he poured his energy into becoming a man worthy of his future wife. I am glad he didn't write a letter like mine… I wouldn't have fit the bill. But I'm grateful that he loves me anyway, flaws and strong-mindedness and all. What a guy!

Jesse: Heidi is too restrained in her praise! When she gave me this letter a few weeks into our relationship, it didn't exactly melt my heart, but I was grateful that she had decided on waiting for the best. This weeded out all the losers she was previously attracted to and let her finally see her dream come true! I truly am the answer to a maiden's prayer!

Wait, let me just empty the rain water out of my nose…

Seriously though, we both had ideas about what we wanted in a future spouse, and in hindsight some of these ideas were not really important. While I never officially wrote out a list, I did have some things that I kept in the back of my mind. I wanted my spouse to be short, dark-haired, and from a large family, preferably near the top of the birth order, and I didn't want to marry an American. God knew what I really wanted and gave me a tall, blond American who was second to last in a relatively small family. Heidi is truly everything I ever hoped for in a spouse. She has only ever exceeded my expectations for a wife. I'm glad I didn't write out such a list or hold my ideas too strongly; I would have missed out on my incredible treasure.

I said earlier that being the right person is more important than finding the right person. While that is true, there are definitely certain types of people who will make it much easier to be the right person! In other words, there are some very important qualities to look for in a spouse. Thankfully, these critical qualities can usually be seen at a distance; you shouldn't need to enter an experimental relationship to check for them. Decide beforehand what you need in a spouse and stick to it!

When deciding, look for strength of character and virtues. Other things such as height, hair color, birth order, taste in movies, music, food, etc., should be negotiable because God knows far better than you what you really need. But there should be areas that you deem absolutely essential. I would like to suggest some items for that list

A CLOSE WALK WITH GOD

Selfishness is poison to a marriage. A person who lives only for himself will be a lifelong chain around your neck. A self-centered person will not care to learn how to communicate or seek to be understanding. Unfortunately, self-centeredness is our default setting since the fall of mankind. There is a constant pull within us to become obsessed with ME. Only surrender to God and the empowering of the Holy Spirit can break the chains of self-centeredness. This is why it is so important that you not only marry a so-called "Christian", but specifically someone who has a genuine humility and dependence upon God. Jesus said that without Him we can do nothing. (John 15:5) When you face the challenges of morning sickness, headaches, crying babies, boredom, and stress, love and romance do not come easily.

There is something about romantic feelings that make us more naturally selfless. When you are infatuated, it is easy to be considerate and show extra courtesies. But when those feelings wear off, or at least take a temporary leave of absence, you will need something deeper to rely on to keep the marriage strong. Learn to be filled with God's love, but also seek to make sure that the person you marry knows how to rely on God's strength.

Spiritual intimacy is one of the strongest binding agents between a husband and wife, but it can only be had if you're both communing with God. The closer you both are to God the closer you will be to each other. I cannot overemphasize the necessity of this point. Every couple who gets married has dreams of their relationship lasting forever, but the friction of two sinful people living together has a terrible power to drive them apart. It is only by the grace and power of God that you will be able to love each other the way you should. Don't compromise or lower your standards in this area: It is vital that your husband or wife be surrendered to God. He or she will not be able to fully give themselves to you unless they have first given their life to God.

A COMPATIBLE LIFE CALLING

In singleness, it may be easy to think about marriage as the be-all-end-all, partly because this is how the fairy tale ends: The hero and heroine get married and live happily ever after. But marriage is not the end. It is a means to the end. Your life purpose is not marriage. God may bring marriage to you, but only to make you more effective in fulfilling your calling.

Knowing your life's calling should play a huge role in your choice of life partner. Your driving motivation in life should not be marriage, but to fulfill the role God has created you to play. I said earlier that any two people who are committed to each other's well-being and enabled by God can make love and romance work. But this does not mean we should feel free to marry whoever we wish. It is so critical that we diligently seek God's advice on this momentous decision.

One of the key issues to consider when making your choice of life partner is to ask, "Does this person have a similar vision for their life purpose? Will he or she distract or hinder me from fulfilling my calling, or help me more effectively reach my God-given goals?"

God brought Heidi into my life because we are more effective serving together. When she sent my article back full of red ink, I was thrilled to see that she was such a great editor and that she loved to write. I had a desire to write, but didn't feel very confident in my abilities. I saw that we could be a great team. It is awesome to see how our strengths in writing complement each other. Heidi has a knack for writing fresh, creative prose, and has a colorful vocabulary (**Heidi:** not sure how to interpret that one…). She also has an eye for grammar and is a champion speller; I am really good at turning on the computer and pressing the space key. Together we make beautiful works of art with depth.

Because we both love writing and can relate to the stresses and difficulties that are involved, we are more understanding of each other. During our second year of marriage, Heidi spent a lot of long hours writing a book about her sister Katrina, who struggled with an eating disorder, and committed suicide when Heidi was seventeen. We had so many late night discussions regarding different angles to take and issues to address, as well as a lot of tears for Heidi as she revisited some very painful memories.

Neither of us complains when the other has a burst of inspiration late at night, or comes late to a meal because we were in the middle of a thought that just had to get put down on paper. We can sympathize with each other's writer's block and the mental fatigue that hits after a long day of writing. We challenge each other to pursue our calling in this area rather than complain about the sacrifices made by the one who is not writing. I am grateful our giftings are so compatible in this area.

Our similar life visions expanded after we got married, and we adopted each other's passions. Heidi has a heart to help bring freedom to girls who struggle with depression and eating disorders and are in bondage to society's lies about beauty and worth. Hearing Heidi talk about her passion and seeing how many girls struggle in these areas has given me a heart for them as well. I am willing to do whatever I can to enable Heidi to serve these girls. I try to support her as she prepares talks or writes articles because her burden for these girls has become mine as well.

Conversely, Heidi has adopted my passion for apologetics and sees the need to have young people equipped in knowing how to seek and defend the truth. Since we've gotten married, God has also given us both a real earnest desire to help young people pursue purity in their relationships and discover the riches of blessings that can be found in holiness and godly romance.

Heidi's been a tremendous encouragement to me in staying faithful to my calling and I hope that I inspire her to do the same. (**Heidi:** You sure do, hon!) I am so grateful for a wife who wants above all else to be right where God wants us. She has put up with many long hours on the road traveling to speaking engagements and lived with my pre-speaking nausea and jitters. She's stood behind me, inspiring me to greater zeal to go wherever God leads us.

Moral purity

A marriage will only work successfully if there is commitment to fidelity. God's design is one man and one woman. If you add an intruder to the equation, it will destroy the marriage. I'm not just talking about a physical affair. If a man is lusting after pornography or fantasizing about other women, he is bringing them into the marriage, and true intimacy will be prevented. If a woman is dressing immodestly and seeking the approval and attention of other men, she is adding them to the equation and will bring ruin. God loves His children so deeply and wants to spare them the pain and destruction that sin brings. He urges us to flee sexual immorality (1 Corinthians 6:18).

When looking for a spouse, make moral purity an absolute requirement. Don't excuse moral impurity, saying that it's no big deal. Girls, please hold out for a man who guards his eyes. A man who doesn't think twice about ogling a pretty young lady or makes suggestive comments about a woman's figure has fallen prey to some destructive lies that will sabotage true intimacy. What you need is a man who's willing to sacrifice himself for you and put your needs ahead of his own. A wandering eye reveals a guy's self-serving attitude concerning his sexuality as well as an inability to control his lust. A man who does not guard his eyes is also letting the culture define what is beautiful and no real woman can hope to compete with computer-altered images. If you are stuck with a husband who lets his eyes run free, you will never feel like you satisfy him.

On the flip side, men are simple and if you tell them something is beautiful they will believe you. If you look throughout history, what men have considered the ideal female shape has changed continually. This is good news for you. If you can find a husband who revels only in your beauty, then as you change shapes throughout the course of your life – either from pregnancy or aging – his tastes will change right along with you and he will always be satisfied by you. But if he lets his eyes roam, then there will be a little dagger in your heart every time you see him lusting after another woman. I've heard so many women share how painful it is to have a husband with wandering eyes. Don't bring this pain upon yourself; don't tell yourself it doesn't matter.

And girls, if you want a guy who will keep his eyes only for you, dress modestly. When you dress in a way that highlights your curves and draws attention to your body, you'll be attracting men with eye problems and driving away the men who are guarding their eyes. You want men to notice you, not just your body. Your beauty is such a precious gift! Don't give it to any jerk who can drool over you like a piece of meat and then walk away. Don't make yourself cheap. Save your beauty for the man who will cherish you, work to provide for you, rub your back while you are throwing up with morning sickness, help to care for and cuddle your babies – the man who will save his eyes for you only. He's the only one who deserves to enjoy your sacred gift.

Please, hold out for a man who does all he can to keep himself pure for you!

Honesty

It's absolutely vital that the person you marry knows how to be honest with you and with himself. Lying and deception will prevent the possibility of intimacy. God is very serious about liars; His Word is full of warnings about them. Proverbs 12:22 says, "The Lord detests lying lips, but He delights in men who are truthful." (NIV) People who develop a habit of lying to others start to lie to themselves as well. A person who uses deception must be avoided at all costs. Don't treat lying casually! Deal with it severely, in yourself as well as in others.

Honesty is more than just avoiding deliberate deception, though. It is also actively making sure that we are accurately communicating our thoughts and feelings. Many people are afraid to let others know how they feel or what is bothering them. Instead they secretly stew over things and become bitter. For intimacy to form, it's so important that both people know how to be honest about their hurts or frustrations. If a spouse is not honest about what he or she is feeling, it's difficult for the other person to guess what is wrong, and the couple will have trouble working through the conflict. Relationship has been defined as "conflict between two people." Without honesty, you won't be able to work through the inevitable conflicts you'll face, and you'll have to live with devastating consequences.

In marriage, you need someone you can trust to be truthful and open. You'll have no idea where you stand with a liar. Intimacy is found in knowing and in being known; lies prevent both from happening. Make sure that when you enter a serious relationship, the other person has demonstrated that he has the ability to be honest with himself and with you, even when the truth stings. Deception will destroy your relationship.

QUALITY RELATIONSHIPS WITH FAMILY.

There is a dirty little secret about marriage: The person you were dating becomes family after you're married. And the way your spouse treated their own family will be the way he or she will treat you. In marriage, the dating games and Friday evening polish-up start to wear off and your lover's true character will bleed through. His habits of interaction with his family will dictate the way he interacts with you. If he tended to be rude and short-tempered with his sisters, then you'd better prepare to be spoken to the same way. If he didn't know where the washer and dryer were at home, don't expect him to be a big help with the laundry.

Guys, be especially watchful of how a young woman speaks about her father. Does she speak of him with respect, or is she nit-picky and belittling? One thing we men have a strong need for from our women is respect and affirmation – with these, we are empowered to be real men and conquer the world. Without these, it's easy to have the life sucked right out of us. This need is so strong that it is often the reason for affairs. Most of the time, the man doesn't run away with another woman because she is more beautiful than his wife, but because she shows him more respect and affirmation. Don't get me wrong – respect needs to be earned and men are not justified in being immoral or weaklings if their wives don't give them the affirmation they need. But the difference between having a critical wife and an affirming wife will be a huge factor in your becoming the kind of man you want to be.

I am very grateful for Heidi; she is so encouraging and appreciative. I can't tell you just how inspiring her words are to me. I knew how much I needed encouraging words from my wife and didn't think I could handle a wife with a critical spirit. It wasn't that I wanted flattery from her or that I didn't want to hear the truth about things I needed to work on. I just knew the power a woman has to build up or tear down. If you look for the good in a person you will find it, but you will also find the negative if you look for it. When a woman makes the choice to be affirming and appreciative, she will see her husband in a much better light than if she has a critical, ungrateful spirit. When I heard girls criticize or belittle their father, or saw them frequently rolling their eyes at the things he did or said, I kept my heart far away from them. Of course, this advice does not just apply to the guys. We all need affirmation and are wounded by criticism. Girls, the same applies to you, look for a guy who knows how to be affirming and stay far, far away, from a man who uses his tongue like a knife.

INNER BEAUTY

Whenever I pictured my future spouse, the woman I imagined was always beautiful. When our family took trips and I was on the lookout for a potential Mrs. Jesse Jost among the people we met along the way, beauty was at the top of the list of absolute requirements. If Mom suggested someone to me that I thought was less than attractive, I quickly found reasons to dismiss the idea. I realize now that I had a very immature perspective on beauty. True beauty is so much deeper than what you can see in a picture.

Don't misunderstand where I'm going with this. Beauty is God's idea. He loves beauty and when He brings the right person into your life, I can guarantee you will find that person beautiful. While an outwardly pretty face is a bonus, it is the character and selflessness that makes a person really beautiful in the way you will appreciate the most. It's really easy to assume that if a person looks great on the outside, they are also sweet and selfless on the inside. Sometimes that is true, but oftentimes outer beauty can mask character flaws.

Outer beauty does not guarantee a great relationship. Just look at the land of the beautiful – Hollywood. The men and women there have faces and bodies that we ordinary people can only dream of having, and yet it is a place full of broken relationships, loneliness, and heartache. It says in the book of Proverbs that "what is desired in a man is kindness" (Proverbs 19:22). The older I get, the more I see just how true that is. What makes for a truly satisfying relationship is two people who are focused on each other instead of stuck on themselves, looking for ways to serve each other, and quick both to ask for forgiveness and to grant it. People who are gentle, compassionate, understanding, joyful, loving, and sensitive – these are the people who are truly beautiful no matter how many beauty pageants would overlook them. Contrary to the cynical wags, the idea that beauty is on the inside is not just something ugly people say. It is true. A smiling, plain face that conveys warmth and care is much more beautiful than a pouty, cold, uncaring expression on a cover model.

Men are especially slow to get this. They just seem to be suckers for a pretty face, even when they have been burned time and time again by a pretty-outside-ugly-inside woman. Guys, you may think a big part of marriage is sex and that a beautiful woman equals great intimacy. It's tempting to think that if you have a beautiful wife, you'll have great sex and, therefore, a great marriage. It's not so simple as that; look at how many beautiful women get divorced. Great sex is the result of having an open and honest relationship with your wife. Intimacy will only be satisfying in the context of selflessness and giving.

What really satisfies me after four years of marriage is not so much the physical side; that is simply the cake's icing – albeit terrific icing! No, what truly satisfies me is having a spiritual and emotional bond with my wife. Heidi is a gorgeous woman, but what makes her such a great wife is who she is on the inside and what she does to serve me. It's her backrubs when I'm sore and tired. It's the way she listens uncritically when I'm working through doubts or anxieties. It's the way I can trust her completely to keep her heart for me only. It's how she goes out of the way to add little touches to things to make life special. It's the warmth from her smiles that gives me tingly feelings, not merely the fact that she would look great on a TV commercial. In fact, I have a confession to make... and I know it sounds stupid. Until just before we started our relationship, I did not find Heidi attractive. It wasn't that I thought she was ugly – I just didn't think she was my type. But when I started falling in love with her because of who she was as a person, the more beautiful she became in my eyes. Now I can honestly say she is the most beautiful woman in the world to me. There have been countless times since then, when I've been gazing at Heidi and marveling, "Wow, she is such a flawless beauty! How did I not see it before?"

Ask God to help you see past externals and find someone who has inner beauty. If you aim for inner beauty, you will get outer beauty thrown in as well. If you aim for outer beauty, you may get neither. A pretty face and great measurements will turn ugly if the inside is poisoned by self-centeredness.

MAKE A WISE CHOICE

These things that I have mentioned above are very important to look for in a spouse; they will make or break a relationship. If your potential mate lacks any of these qualities listed above, please seriously consider whether you should progress deeper into the relationship. These things can be learned eventually, but they are vital to a successful marriage. When a spouse lacks one of these qualities, it'll cause serious problems in your marriage. Please don't let charm or a pretty face deceive you. Make these character traits a must in what you are looking for, and make sure that you are developing them in yourself as well.

Maybe you are in a position where you think a person might be right for you. He or she has great character and is a good friend, but you are holding back because you don't feel a lot of spark or romantic feelings for this person. Don't let that be the deciding factor. I want to make this clear. Romantic feelings can be created in the context of commitment! Feelings come and go. Couples who have made it for the long haul will tell you that there are many times in marriage where the feelings leave, yet they've been able to bring romantic feelings back, even after a long period of absence.

There was a long time prior to our relationship when I felt no romantic attraction to Heidi, but when I made the choice to win her heart, I fell madly in love with her. And because at first I was a klutz, Heidi lost all romantic feelings for me. But we kept working at our friendship and serving each other, and the romantic passion ended up consuming both of us. Now it may be you don't have feelings because you don't sense God's leading; that is a different story. But if all the other pieces are in place and your only concern is that there's no spark, don't worry. Romantic attraction can be learned.

The decision of life partner is perhaps one of the biggest decisions you will ever make. Ruled by the clear guidelines of God's Word, your mind should make the decision, not your easily blinded, infatuated heart. Make a wise decision! When you begin enjoying love God's way, you will have bound yourself to a woman or man for life. You cannot tear away without terrible consequences. When you've made a decision, stick with it. When you face difficulties, don't start asking, "Is this the right person? Should I dump her?" No! Now is the time for you to begin being the right person.

Let me add, though, something that has amazed me. When you trust God's timing and let Him guide you in the choice of life partner, He will simply blow you away with a perfect match. I didn't know Heidi that well experientially on the day that I committed to her. I did see that she met the important requirements that I just mentioned and that she was the girl God wanted me to marry. Life with her has been one pleasant surprise after another; I couldn't have created a better friend if I tried. God knew exactly what I needed. Our tastes are so similar in the music we like, the movies we watch, the food we enjoy, what we find funny. I just can't get over what a perfect fit we are, and I am so grateful that I did not have to date lots of women to find her.

CHAPTER 6

SEE YOUR FAMILY AS A TRAINING SCHOOL FOR MARRIAGE

Like I said earlier, your spouse will become family, and the habits you are forming now in the way you treat your family will dictate how you'll treat your spouse. Obviously there are some areas of your future marriage that you won't be able to prepare for as a single person, but there are many other aspects of a successful relationship that you can be working on right now.

Your family provides you with a great training school for marriage. You can learn so many valuable things about communication, patience, servanthood, selfless love, repentance, and forgiveness. Marriage can be the sweetest relationship in the world, but if you get married I guarantee you will be marrying another fallen human being. You may expect married life to be one long, blissful fairy tale, but in reality marriage has just as many relationship difficulties as you find at home, if not more. If you often fight with your siblings or parents, don't expect your relationship with your spouse to be much different. If you can't communicate with your family, don't expect a honeymoon to magically transform you.

On the other hand, if you can learn to say you were wrong and apologize to an ugly, overbearing brother (and I don't speak from experience here), where the only reward is hearing him say, "I told you I was right," just think how much easier it will be to apologize to a beautiful wife who lovingly forgives and may reward you with a long hug and a kiss!

Here are some things you can work on now that will pay huge dividends later.

SERVANTHOOD

In my years of being married, I have found that I feel most in love when I am serving Heidi in some way. I can be a pretty selfish person and am often self-absorbed, but when I heed the Spirit's promptings and find ways to serve Heidi, such as doing the dishes or giving her a foot rub, I am filled with so much joyful love. It's baffling that when I think about serving, my flesh groans, "not again!" I would much rather be served than serve. But this natural reaction is such a puzzle to me because I always feel so happy and fulfilled while serving! From what I've heard, that's true for most people. Yet we still tend to act on our inclination to be served rather than to serve. Go figure!

In marriage, when both spouses are expecting to be served or keeping score of how the other is not serving properly, there will be discord and a general dissatisfaction with the marriage. Conversely, when they're both seeking ways to serve each other, they both find satisfaction.

If you're single, you obviously don't have a spouse who can serve you, but you do have many opportunities to serve your family and friends. Take advantage of this, and look for creative ways you can bless someone. If you get in the habit of serving, not only will you be far more fulfilled as a single person, you will also be growing a root system that will bear the satisfying fruits of a very happy marriage.

REPENTANCE AND FORGIVENESS

Many people have said that good communication is the most important element to a successful marriage. A good case can be made for that, but I tend to agree with novelist Walter Wangerin, Jr., who says that forgiveness is the most important thing in a good marriage. The kind of intimacy involved in a good marriage requires that you show the most sensitive side of your soul. This kind of vulnerability with each other can be rewarding, but sometimes also painful. I'm embarrassed by how sensitive I've been about little things that Heidi has done or said. She meant no harm, but they still hurt and I felt like a baby for being pricked by such minor things. I chide myself that I need to be a man. But I also realize that to have true intimacy with Heidi, I need to take my armor – my protective shell – off or I will be insensitive to her needs and wants. I grew up with seven brothers. I knew how to keep my guard up and not be an oversensitive wimp around them. But it is so different with Heidi. With her I want to be completely open and vulnerable; I want to share deep intimate love, but that involves pain.

From an outsider's perspective, couples split up over small issues. You may not realize that even though these things seem insignificant, to lovers they can wound deeply. A slash with a knife to calloused skin will not hurt as much as a minor scrape to sensitive skin.

The only way to be free of this emotional pain is to be free of love, and that is hell. I know I have hurt my precious Heidi often with my own thoughtless words and actions, and knowing I have hurt her is worse pain than when I have been hurt. Some couples deal with their hurt by putting their armor back on and moving apart, which only forces them deeper into themselves, intensifying their loneliness. We have a built-in need for open intimacy, but it will hurt – there is no way around it. That's why learning to forgive is so important. If you don't learn to forgive and let go, these small issues will accumulate, becoming heavy weights around your neck. Every time your spouse commits the same offense, the weight of the times he committed it in the past will come crashing down on you and it'll be a harder blow every time.

One of the most painful ways to die is by a blocked bowel. When the body doesn't know how to process and let go of its waste, it becomes poisoned to death. It is the same way with a marriage – waste is the natural by-product of two fallen humans living with each other. You'll have to learn how to deal with the hazardous waste in conflict if you want the marriage to stay healthy. This means learning how to admit you were wrong and asking forgiveness, letting go of certain things and leaving them in the past. To be able to do this, you must learn to give the hurt and pain to God and let Him bring healing. You have to trust that God is in control and is using people's wrong choices for good in your life. Learning to forgive involves learning to see God's hand in everything. Right now, in your family relationships, are you becoming a bitter, easily offended person? Or do you know how to bring these offenses to God and let Him deal with them? If you let God take care of things, you will be free and will have the makings of an excellent spouse.

GENTLENESS

Like I mentioned above, true love results in heightened sensitivity. Guys, it is especially important that you learn right now to control your tongue. It's easy to spout off harsh words and vent your anger. In the locker room, such tirades may not do much damage, but to the soft, sensitive soul of your wife, these words can cut like a knife. Guys and girls, when you and your spouse are sorting through the inevitable conflict, sharp or terse words or words delivered with a raised voice will increase the tension and anger and make resolution much harder to attain. "Harsh words stir up anger" (Proverbs 15:1).

I'm not telling you to stuff your feelings for fear of being harsh. When negative feelings are stored away, your spouse will not be able to help you deal with them. Soon these bottled up feelings will explode, causing great damage. You need to learn how to deal with your anger and frustration in a gentle and controlled way. "A soft answer turns away wrath" (Proverbs 15:1). View the conflicts you have with your friends or siblings as opportunities to learn self-control and gentleness with your tongue. I know that this can be hard to do. Sadly, we often treat our family with less respect than we treat strangers. Sharp words can be a habit, but they don't have to be. Cry out to God for the grace to help you control your tongue;

it will save your spouse a lot of heartache.

AFFIRMATION

I believe that affirmation is one of the most important elements in keeping love alive. Much is said about the damage words can bring, but little is said about the great good that can come from choice words. "Death and life are in the power of the tongue and those who love it will eat its fruit" (Proverbs 18:21). Words of encouragement, appreciation, and affirmation are life-giving! They can soften your spouse's heart, tearing down the defenses that prevent intimacy. Each of us battles insecurity to one degree or another, and this lack of confidence can lead to withdrawal and inhibitions where love is concerned, but encouraging words give us the confidence we need to love freely.

Positive affirmation inspires us to try harder and be even more diligent in the area we were praised. Critical, negative comments can take the wind right out of our sails and make us want to give up. Spouses who criticize each other tear down the motivation to even try repairing their love. However, if a spouse takes a small step to build up the marriage – maybe an act of service, a kind gesture, or some tender affection – and this step is met with appreciation, he or she will be inspired to take more steps.

There is another aspect to this as well. Our perception of each other is very limited and prone to error. We rarely see things in their entirety. In fact, we have a tendency to see what we expect to see, and miss the rest. When you make the choice to be affirming and look for things to praise in your spouse, you will see many positive things to fill you with gratitude. But, thanks to the help of our unseen enemy, if you follow the path of least resistance, you will tend toward negativity, and Satan is only too happy to point out all the flaws in your spouse. If you look for the bad, you will see it, and neither you nor your spouse will be very satisfied with each other. This choice of focus – to be either critical or affirming – will be a huge swing factor in whether or not you have a happy marriage. Right now, with your family, are you forming habits of praise and affirmation? Or negativity and a critical spirit? The choice is yours.

FAMILY IS PRECIOUS

The secret to a successful relationship is being filled with Christ's selfless agape love. Your relationship with your family is an excellent test of what kind of relationship you will have with your spouse. If this section has sobered you, remember that it is never too late to begin anew in your relationships. If you don't have a family nearby, remember you can still use the close relationships you do have with roommates or co-workers to practice the skills that will give you a successful marriage. Invest in your future spouse by investing in your family right now.

But remember, your family should be treated right not merely so you can practice becoming a better spouse! Each member of your family is worthy of your love and respect in their own right. As a single person, you should treasure these relationships. Don't treat them lightly. No one ever regretted investing more into relationships with his or her family, but many have wept regretfully that they let something so precious slip away.

CHAPTER 7

BE OPEN WITH YOUR PARENTS

Until you are a parent yourself, you can't fully imagine what it's like to love a little person so deeply and be willing to do anything for that precious child. I'll never forget what it was like to become a father. This is the letter I sent out a week after John-Michael was born; it captures some of the emotions new parents have.

WARNING: LOTS OF PROUD PAPA PONTIFICATION TO FOLLOW!

Right now I am holding in my arms one of the most beautiful babies ever born. Of course, I am biased because this little angel is my own. That's right, John-Michael Jesse was born on January 15, 2007, weighing in at 8 lbs. 14 oz., He and I have much in common: lots of dark hair, very intelligent, we both think Heidi is the most beautiful woman in the world, and we both entered the world looking like we took a wrong turn at Neptune.

The baby's due date was Jan. 7. The ultrasound put the date at Dec. 29, but we were just married on March 25, so we knew our dates! We waited and waited for this little one to poke his head out. Finally the doctor scheduled an induction on the 15th. We were really praying that Heidi wouldn't have to be induced. Talk about cutting it close! On the night of the 14th Heidi had some mild, albeit regular contractions. Early the next morning, the nurse told us over the phone that it didn't sound like Heidi was in labor yet and to come on in for the induction. Well, the real labor started just as Heidi was about to be induced, so the doctor decided not to. Whew!

Our exhilaration was tempered by the immediate onslaught of intense labor. The contractions came hard and heavy for hours. Then, when this little rascal finally decided to enter this world, Heidi and I looked down at the hairy, purple, slimy mass on the bed, then looked at each other with shock and said, "It's a boy!" We had thought for sure that it was a girl.

This precious baby has filled our home with so much joy! I am overwhelmed with gratitude to God for His amazing gift. It almost hurts to love someone this much. I love being a dad. I must admit that I had several selfish thoughts during the past nine months, because I love Heidi and just being the two of us has been so fun; the freedom and flexibility to do whatever we want has been great. So I was a little apprehensive about how the baby's arrival would change things... I'd forgotten how love changes things. Our first night out of the hospital, we stayed with my grandparents. I had to sleep on the floor. At 2:30 am, Heidi woke me up to walk the baby. I had just finally gotten into a deep sleep and it took a while to get oriented. I reached for a light and spilled a glass of water all over me and my sleeping bag. "Welcome to the world of being a daddy!" I thought. But as I sat with John-Michael on the couch and gazed at the face of our rapidly-becoming-cute newborn, the wonder of it all sank in just a little bit more. It's hard to describe the rush of love that you feel for your own child until you actually experience it.

Just before we left the hospital, I felt a little scared about taking this little one out into the world and the new challenges we would face. But as I stepped outside with our luggage, the world looked different. I was struck with an overwhelming thought, "I'm a father!" I straightened my back and stood up a little taller. My apprehensive feelings fell away into the background. What mattered was that I had a wife and son to take care of. Whatever life threw at us, I had a whole new courage and resolve to face it; I would not let my family down.

Heidi and I have just been in seventh heaven since we came home. John-Michael has been an absolute dream baby! His studious eyes and expressions when he's awake and little smiles and coos that he makes when he's asleep totally melt our hearts. In short, we LOVE being parents! Thank you all so much for praying for us. We can't wait to show him off!

I shared this to hopefully help you catch a glimpse of just how much your parents care for you and want your best in the area of romance, even though it may seem at times like they are out of touch with what's hip, or worse, you see them as jail guards who work overtime to keep you from fun. Many of them have been praying for your future spouse since the day you were born. Once you become a parent yourself, you will realize how deeply your own parents love you and how earnestly they desire what is best for you. If you open up your heart to them and invite them into this process of discovering what God has for you and look to them for guidance and counsel, you may find them to be wonderful allies and a great source of strength.

The infatuation safeguard

It can be very challenging to guard your heart while single. An attractive, godly member of the opposite gender can send your mind floating into daydream-land. Sleeping hearts often dream. What can you do when you find your heart thumping and your brain wearing out its cells replaying video and audio clips of Mr. or Miss Incredible?

Heidi and I found that the most effective way to battle infatuation (and believe me, we did have to battle it!) was to be very open and honest with our parents.

Anytime I developed a strong attraction to some godly young lady, I would share that with my mom. It was easier to share my romantic interests with Mom. When I was younger, Dad would tease me about girls, so I didn't feel as comfortable talking with him about my infatuations. However, Dad was the one to whom I told all my sexual temptations and confessions. He was always so understanding and reassuring.

Sharing these feelings of infatuation brought them out into the light, and made them so much easier to deal with. The romantic heart is easily deceived and love is blind. Being honest with my mom brought much protection. It was so helpful to have Mom remind me of principles that I had lost sight of and to know that she and Dad loved me a lot and really wanted what was best for me. She always spoke of romance as a special, sacred thing, beautiful in its proper time. I felt safe sharing my heart because she never made light of my feelings. She listened with kindness and compassion, but her love also had a firm quality to it; she wasn't afraid to gently show me where my thinking had gone wrong. Mom frequently prayed with me about my struggles and also for my future spouse. During these prayer times, I often found the strength and inspiration I needed to guard my heart.

The wisdom of years

Your parents can provide so much protection. They can help prevent you from making some of the same mistakes they have made. You know how it is said that hindsight is 20/20? Your parents are farther down the road; they have the wisdom of hindsight to offer you. They've been through a lot more of life, and have seen the consequences different actions can reap. When they counsel you to refrain from doing certain things, it's likely because they have an insight that you don't yet have. I'm sure they only have your best in mind. They want you to enjoy life and be richly satisfied.

In your choice of life partner, your parents can be a huge help. They will often be a better judge of character than you will, because they won't be blinded by stunningly gorgeous appearances, or by hormones that have just gone wacky. Ask them for guidance and counsel. They'll be able to see things that you will miss, and can be an invaluable source of wisdom in the situations you face.

God often chooses to lead through the parents' guidance. If you really want God to direct your love life, then invite your parents into your evaluating and decision-making processes. When they give you a red light or caution you, pay attention! They may not always be right, but God has the power to change their hearts if they are wrong. Trust God to be able to lead you through your parents.

We realize that not everyone is blessed with godly parents that you can confide in, and some of you have lost your parents through divorce, broken relationships, or death. But you can still seek out a godly mentor with whom you can be open. Ask God to give you a close relationship with a spiritually and morally strong relative or church leader. We all need the protection and wisdom of someone older and more mature than us. It is so easy to get caught up in the follies of youth. Sharing your struggles and desires with a wise mentor will give you the proper perspective you need.

We can learn and benefit from our parents' (or mentor's) wisdom and in doing so, spare ourselves a lot of pain and heartache. Satan wants each generation to feel like they have to figure things out for themselves. There is no need to start out with a blank slate and be forced to make all the same mistakes that previous generations made! You can learn from your parents so that you have a head start in achieving the goal of a regret-free life.

I'm not at all saying you need to let your parents make all your decisions. You are responsible for your own choices and you need to know how to be decisive. However, it is wise to seek your parents' guidance. When you do, they'll probably be open and honest; most likely, they will be so blessed you asked. Together, you can work toward a terrific future. This doesn't mean that you remain a child who is completely dependent on them for everything; that kind of unhealthy dependency can harm your marriage. I'm talking about a healthy friendship of trust and openness. I'm guessing your parents want you to become a healthy independent adult as much as you do. However, if they see you making foolish decisions and shunning their counsel, their desire to protect you will probably make them feel the need to be even more invasive and controlling. On the other hand, if they see that you are teachable and willing to listen, they'll likely be more willing to release you. It's ironic, but dependence on your parents' counsel can be the path to independence and freedom.

A HEAD START IN UNDERSTANDING

There's another benefit of sharing your feelings with your parents besides receiving the wisdom and protection they can offer. Being open with your mom and dad is wonderful preparation for learning how to be open with your future spouse.

There have been so many rewards that have come from my learning to be open with Mom. I learned much about how to serve her, give her encouragement, and how to understand her (as much as any guy can understand a woman). The things I gleaned from my relationship with Mom have paid huge dividends in my relationship with Heidi. It has been easy to share my thoughts, feelings, dreams, and fears because I had learned to do that with Mom. Heidi has mentioned many times her gratefulness for the closeness I had with my mom.

Heidi: Similarly, during my last year at home, I really worked at building a closer relationship with my dad. It finally clicked in my mind that – wow, here I had a priceless opportunity to be a daughter who could offer her dad support and encouragement. He was carrying a lot of burdens at the time, and I just wanted to be there to listen to whatever he wanted to share, and to affirm him as much as I could. He had to make several trips from our farm to town for business every week, so I often went along for the 40-minute drive. I came to really enjoy these daddy-daughter times, whether or not we talked much. After years of being pretty absorbed with my own thoughts and feelings and less aware of my dad's, I found it really satisfying to reach out more and give to him. And I realized more than ever what an amazing father I had.

Jesse: I'm sure her dad loved the change and the increased interaction, but I feel like I am the one who has benefited most from that choice. Heidi entered marriage skilled in knowing how to support and inspire her man. You have that opportunity as well. One of the key ways you can prepare for marriage is by working on your relationship with your parents. The skills in communication and understanding that you gain from your relationship with your parents will help you lay a strong foundation for you and your spouse.

ITS A GIRL!!

I want to close this chapter with another birth announcement. Our home is once again filled with the sweet sounds and smells of a newborn and the uncontainable burst of love that fills the soul. Last week, another precious little angel landed in our world at 9:42 am on September 7, 2009. Sophia Josephine weighed in at 8 lbs. 4 oz., 21.5 inches. Right now as I type, Sophia, wearing a pink shirt and adorable pink floral pants with little ruffles across the bottom, is nestled against my chest sleeping. Like her brother, she is so cute. (In the looks department, I still can't get over how much Heidi was able to do with what I gave her to work with.) The love that grips me when I'm holding my very own daughter splits my heart with unbelievable force. I am filled with a driving passion to do whatever it takes to protect this sweetheart. I desperately want to spare her the heartache that has haunted so many young women. Girls, you have no idea the love a father feels when he's given his own tiny little daughter. I don't know if your father has the ability to express to you how much he loves you. But I do know that you are precious to him. He wants what is best for you. Give him your heart and you will find your daddy to be a place of great refuge.

WHEN DADDIES GO BAD...

If you do not have a dad who treats you with love and respect but is abusive verbally or physically, I hurt for you and your father. I can't imagine how much pain your father must have gone through to twist him and cause him to override his God-given drive to protect and cherish you. Let me assure you that you do have a loving Father in heaven who is watching over you and can bring beauty from the terrible pain He has allowed you to go through. Even though it may not seem like it at times, God really does care for you and He has the power to bring healing into your life. The wrongs you have experienced make Him angry and the men who have abused you will pay the consequences.

In the meantime, let God be your Father. Bring Him all your anger and tears. Vent on His shoulder. Yes, I'm sure you have a lot of hurt and feelings of blame you want to cast on God for not protecting you. However, walking away from God will not solve your problems. It will only make them worse. God let His only Son experience abuse and shame and torture so that you could find healing and, someday, a world without pain. Ask God to be the loving Father you so desperately need and seek out a godly older man whom you can trust and let him be a source of guidance and protection. If you let Him, God can restore you physically and emotionally. God can use the hurts you have gone through to cause healing in the lives of other girls who have been through similar trials. Don't give up on God or on people. It is amazing the changes for good that God's grace can bring.

Chapter 8

BUILD HEALTHY NON-ROMANTIC RELATIONSHIPS

While you're single, I believe it's important to learn how to have healthy relationships with the opposite gender, to know how to talk to them without blundering or stuttering. You need to know how to be sensitive to the differences between the sexes. But I think you can learn how to have these relationships without pairing off into an exclusive, romantic realm.

Being around other guys or girls in a proper environment allows you to learn valuable skills for social interaction and to get to know them as friends. It's critical that you know the person you may someday commit to, and wholesome friendships make that possible. Have fun doing things in groups or as families.

I've read a few books that advocate "wise casual dating" for singles and simultaneously caution that emotional boundaries need to be put in place. While I agree about the importance of young people learning how to have a healthy relationship with the opposite gender, I think it's naïve to believe these young people can pair up in exclusive relationships while keeping emotional distance. Married couples understand the powerful pull between a man and a woman and often put in safeguards for protection. That's why a wife doesn't feel comfortable with her husband being alone in a vehicle or house with another woman. Time alone together and the feeling of belonging to another person are fuel for the fires of romance. If married people think it is wise to stay away from such situations, then singles who are even hungrier for romance and more vulnerable would be wise to take heed.

Single people can learn a lot from their married friends and apply similar safety measures. I think of the story of the boy who was frantically waving his arms in the lake and yelling, "I can't swim!" A small boy on the shore simply yelled back, "I can't either, but you don't hear me crying about it!" They had the same weakness, but one boy was drowning because of where he was. All men and women have a propensity to give into sexual or emotional compromise, but the situations you place yourself in will determine whether your purity is maintained or destroyed.

If you still feel there is nothing wrong with casual romantic affection, look at it this way. Suppose you come home one afternoon and you see your mom walking down the street holding hands with a man who is not her husband. Do you think, "Oh, there's nothing wrong with that - holding hands is innocent." Or would a little alarm bell go off in your head?

"Mom, what are you doing?! You belong to Dad!"

What if she responded, "What's wrong with it? I see you doing this all the time with your friends and I don't see any wedding ring on your finger!"

Why does it seem wrong to see your mom giving that kind of affection to another man? Because you instinctively recognize that some kinds of affection should belong solely to a spouse. Our culture's thinking about these things has become so twisted that what should strike us as intuitively wrong now seems "innocent" and "harmless."

If you keep all your interaction with friends of the opposite sex to a level that you would feel comfortable watching your mom or dad have with someone they are not married to, your spouse and your friends' future spouses will be so grateful you did!

WHERE'S THE LINE?

Maybe you wonder about boundaries and exactly when an activity becomes "romance." But Christianity is not about laws that tell us how much we can get away with. Christianity is about being so completely transformed by Christ's love that we do not seek to get as close to temptation as we can, but rather as close to God's best as we are able.

I like the story about the baroness who was interviewing drivers for a chauffeur position. She pointed to the brick wall along her driveway, and asked each one how close they could maneuver her Rolls Royce to the wall without scraping or otherwise damaging the car. The first one said, "Oh, about two feet," and the second one boasted that he could comfortably come within a foot. But the third fellow said, "I don't know, but I would stay as far away as I could." The third one got the job.

As soon as you define love and relationships to be merely about laws and boundaries, people want to see how close they can get to the line. But when you are motivated by genuine love, you seek to love your spouse to the best of your ability. So when you are with another young person, you shouldn't be asking, "How far can we go?" but rather, "What is the best way I can show love to this person and to my future spouse?"

If you really love the young man or woman you are with, you will seek what is best for them. Keep the gift of romantic love and physical intimacy within the safe confines of lifelong commitment. In your relationships, be vigilant that you protect your future spouse, the person you are with, and yourself. Premature, "illegitimate" romance has the potential to deeply hurt all three people.

The satisfaction of contentment

Some of you may feel that cutting the pre-commitment romance out of your life sounds like a drag, but let me tell you it can be so much fun and freeing! When I was single and had a crush on someone, it was miserable! I hated that sick-to-the-pit-of-my-stomach ache, and the discontent it caused. When my heart was asleep, I felt so free!

Building the fires of romantic and physical longings in the context of singleness is a recipe guaranteed to produce frustration or worse. These longings were designed to be culminated in physical intimacy. However, premarital sex is a devastating thing that leaves guilt and emptiness in its wake. So it follows that, outside of marriage, these stirred-up longings will never be fulfilled and you'll be miserably frustrated if they are not kept in check. Unbidden desires for physical intimacy are hard enough to handle, but when you stoke the fire with physical affection, love notes, and emotional bonding – man, are you ever going to make it hard for yourself! That frustration does not sound fun! When your desire for sex has been stoked, you'll be in a "damned if you do, damned if you don't" situation.

Let me tell you, it was so much easier to save sex for marriage because we saved all of romance for each other only. Couples who are trying to save sex for marriage, but are spending time alone cuddling in vehicles, fondling on a couch, or kissing, are begging for disaster or at best, real frustration.

The less you're engaging in romantic activities, the more free you will feel. When you're not blinded by infatuation or feeling the pressure of trying to impress a certain someone, you can find a delicious freedom to enjoy a healthy relationship with other young people. You can begin inspiring each other toward godliness, rather than dragging each other down by defrauding and distracting. As brothers and sisters in Christ, you have a responsibility to love and protect one another. Paul instructs us in Philippians 2:3-4, "Let nothing be done through selfish ambition or conceit, but in lowliness of mind let each esteem others better than himself. Let each of you look out not only for his own interests, but also for the interests of others."

It's natural to want to make other people fall for you. Knowing you are appealing to the opposite gender can feel tremendously good. But once Christ gets hold of you, your first desire should be to protect others and put their needs above your own. These verses need to govern your relationships with other young people.

A man's job: protector, not stealer of hearts

Guys, learn to be a gentleman who treats every girl and woman with courtesy and respect. The world needs examples of men who know how to honor and respect women and show them their true worth. The world's idea of a real man is one who lusts after women, using and degrading them – a far cry from God's ideal! Treat each woman like you would your mother and your sister. If you don't treat your mother and sisters properly, then begin there! As a man, you have a high calling to provide protection for the women and children you encounter. Lay down your life for them right now. Chivalry that is only inspired by infatuation is worthless.

Be sensitive to the emotional vulnerabilities of the women around you. When you flatter young women, give them affectionate touch, such as putting your arm around them, or write them tender words of affirmation, you could be setting their hearts on fire and stirring up untimely desires that will make life hard for them. In the world's view, this is a harmless game young people play to try and get others to fall for them. But that is not a loving thing to do to a sister in Christ! Paul tells us in 1 Thessalonians 4:3-6 that "It is God's will that you should be sanctified: that you should avoid sexual immorality; that each of you should learn to control his own body in a way that is holy and honorable, not in passionate lust like the heathen, who do not know God; and that in this matter no one should wrong his [sister] or take advantage of [her]." (NIV)

Your job as a young man is to protect young women's hearts, not make things more difficult. See yourself not as Casanova the womanizer, but as Great Heart from Pilgrim's Progress, whose job was to safely escort Christiana to her husband. Think about these young ladies' future husbands. Would you be able to look them in the eye, confident that you were completely honorable in striving to protect their precious brides? Or will you look at your feet in shame because you stole from these men?

Protecting young women's hearts does not mean you have to be cold or ignore girls for fear of defrauding them. It is important that you are friendly and cordial. A young woman should feel like she has value to you as a sister. You should be treating all young women equally. If you're being extra courteous and respectful and chivalrous only to attractive girls, you'd better check your motivation. Treat each girl with gentleness and kindness, the way you want other men to be treating your future wife.

A woman's greatest gift: her beauty

Girls, learn how to respect the men in your life and how to inspire them toward greater purity and God-centered focus. As we encouraged earlier, dress modestly to help prevent your weaker brother from stumbling. I want to explain something to you from a man's perspective. God designed men to be turned on by the sight of a woman's body; this is part of the beautiful gift of sex. It's a mystery how the sight of a female body can have such a strong physical effect on a man's body, but that's the way men are wired. If a man sees a sensual body or image, it is like a strong potion producing a powerful wave of desire, especially in single young men who are staying abstinent and do not have an outlet for their sexual desire. This doesn't mean these men are perverted; it is simply the way they were designed, and in marriage, no guy will protest this aspect of our masculinity!

When I was single, I remember accidentally seeing a book cover or a flashed image on an ad, and feeling an ethereal wave of desire, and suddenly I found myself battling a raging fire. I didn't like it, I didn't want it, and I didn't seek it out. I tried to look away as soon as I could, but the damage had still been done. Part of growing up into manhood is learning how to control these urges and not let them destroy us. We are not justified – ever – in giving into lust or letting our eyes stray. We can learn to bounce our eyes, and avoid looking at areas where we know we will be tempted, but we can't change the effect that a woman's body has on us.

I'm not saying we're untamed animals that can't handle being around women. God has made it so that when a woman is dressed modestly, we can look at her as a sister and not as an object of pleasure. Part of God's magnificent design is that only the sight of certain body parts will turn us on. Just about anything between your neck and your knees, if it is made visible, or revealed by clothing that is too tight, is going to have this effect on almost any male who looks at you.

Many women enjoy the sense of power that they exert over men by dressing this way. I'm sure it feels good to know that men find you attractive and that you have North America's number one asset – sex appeal. But think about it - when you dress provocatively, what effect are you having on the men who see you? When you get men's attention and rev up their motors, to some of them you will morph from a human woman with thoughts and feelings to an impersonal object of pleasure, a piece of meat to drool over. Is that the response you want? A godly man is going to be distracted by you and will fight the urge to look at you, and you will set off in him an inner struggle that could produce guilt, alienation from God, or emotional distance from his spouse or future spouse if he gives in and starts to lust after your curves. At best, men will ignore you because they're seeking to stay pure; at worst, you will either defile their mind or be turned in to a sex object.

Is this the effect you are looking for?

You don't have to start wearing sacks or unflattering designs, but there is a clear difference between clothes that conceal and clothes that reveal. You can dress very attractively and still be modest. By modest I mean that you won't trigger sexual arousal in other men. When you dress modestly and feminine, men will see you as very pretty, but it will be in a way that draws their eyes to your face, and helps remind them that you are a real woman with emotions and opinions. Being modest will attract guys to who you are as an individual – the real you – as opposed to a faceless object.

As a godly young woman who has made Christ the Lord of her life, you'll desire to put the needs of others ahead of your own. You can inspire your brothers in Christ to their high calling by being feminine. Set an example to your sisters who are following you of how to dress and how to behave toward young men. You should have a desire to protect the men around you as brothers and be willing to sacrifice for them. Lots of Christian guys keep their guard up when they're "in the world," but they want to be able to just relax and let that guard down for awhile when they are fellowshipping among other Christians. The careless move or revealing outfit of a sister in Christ can take them by surprise and set off a fire of desire and distraction that ruins what could have been a rewarding time for edification or worshipping God.

You don't want to stand before God on Judgment Day and see a long list of brothers you caused to stumble because you wanted to be fashionable. These men will also be held accountable for their lust, but you will grieve that the wonderful gift of your beauty was used to send a fiery dart of the enemy into vulnerable young men. I should warn you that Satan desperately wants to use your body to bring harm. He will be whispering in your ear to keep pushing the limits and inching you toward dressing more sensually, but all the while he will be telling you that you are modest enough, and if guys have trouble with what you're wearing it's their fault. Please don't fall for the lie. For the sake of those around you and for your own protection, be careful how you dress. If you're not sure about an outfit, ask your dad or your brother and they can let you know if it is modest.

Heidi: Girls, if you're still confused about what "modest" means, and wanting a little more help in making your wardrobe modest, you might want to check out www.purefreedom.org/media0015.htm and read Dannah Gresh's modesty guidelines. Note that these guidelines for modesty are available to download as a mini-poster - a great thing to tack up by your closet or bedroom mirror.

THROW AWAY THE DAISIES

Jesse: Here is something else for you girls to consider. As you interact with guys, there will be times where guys are friendly and you will be tempted to spend a lot of mental energy trying to figure out if he has a crush on you or if his care and attention has ulterior motives. You can make things so much easier for yourself by refusing to play the "he likes me, he likes me not" game. Not only is that a waste of mental and emotional energy, but it won't help you or the young man in question. Do yourself a huge favor and don't assume that a young man's courtesy to you is because he's got a crush on you. Until a man spells out his intentions in an unmistakable way and commits to you, then for your own good and his, just assume that he has no intentions toward you and that he belongs to someone else. You will save yourself a lot of heartache! Better to be surprised and find out the young man is interested and committed, than to be continually disappointed.

Heidi: I wish I'd thought of this when I first started noticing and becoming interested in boys. I would have had a lot more brain space (a limited commodity for this blonde) to focus on other more valuable things, like how I was treating my family, and what ways I could serve the people around me. Instead, I wasted plenty of thoughts and time wondering, "Does he like me – or doesn't he?" It would have helped a lot just to assume he didn't, and to redirect all that emotion into heartfelt prayers for his growth in God, etc.

Jesse: Guys or girls, if you find yourself infatuated with a special young person, surrender him/her to God. Begin praying for that person and their future spouse – you never know, you may be praying for yourself. Guys, it's important that you do not communicate your affection until you know that she is someone you are willing to sacrifice your life for. Until you commit to her, protect her like she belongs to someone else. Don't be jealous of her or demand that she keep her affection for you. She does not belong to you until you put a ring on her finger.

FRIENDS WHO PURSUE PURITY

One more thing before we move on. If you want to stay committed and faithful to the ideals that God has shown you, it is vital that you surround yourself with friends who are like-minded. Nothing can chip away at your resolve like peer pressure. Still, if you have just a couple of close friends who share your vision for love, romance, and purity, they will be a tremendous strength to you. I am so grateful for the friendships I had during my teen years. My siblings, cousins, and young people from our church set an example of wholehearted service to Christ and a commitment to obey Him in every area of our life.

Don't try to do this as a lone ranger. You won't make it. I can only imagine how much harder it would have been to stay faithful to my future wife if I was not surrounded by people who held similar convictions and recognized the value of purity. We need the body of Christ and the support they provide. It will be so much easier to implement these truths into your life in the context of a caring community of believers. Ask God to lead you to a group of friends that will provide strength and accountability, friends who are willing to be honest with you and yet speak truth with sensitivity. Obviously we shouldn't only interact with people who hold our convictions; God specifically asks us to shed His light into the lives of those who have different beliefs. But I have seen firsthand just how much we need godly friendships.

If your friends don't see things the way you do, be prepared to boldly yet gently defend your views. If people ask you why you don't have a boyfriend, be prepared with an answer. Often times all you need to do is simply answer that you want the first person you fall in love with to be your future spouse. People will respect that, and may even be envious. Whatever their response, it doesn't matter. You are living for God and your future spouse and you will reap a delicious reward.

Please don't read these admonitions as naggings from a self-righteous, know-it-all prude. I sincerely want to spare you precious people heartache and shame and to see you enjoy the fullness of all God has for you. His rules are empowering, not restrictive burdens.

Chapter 9

LEARN TO COMMUNICATE

COMMUNICATION 101

D rs. Les and Leslie Parrott, in their book *Love Talk*, relay the story of columnist Mark Trahant, and his traditional wedding to a Navaho woman. "As was customary, tribal couples crowded into their Hogan to offer counsel to the newlyweds. One man cleared his throat as if to speak, but at that very moment his wife kneed him in the back. So he kept silent. Later he again cleared his throat but again felt his wife's probing knee. It happened a third time.

"As the guests filed out, the wife with the knee asked her husband, 'Why did you say nothing?'

"'I was going to, but each time I was about to speak, I thought you didn't want me to.'

"'I nudged you three times to get you to speak,' she protested. 'What would you have said?'

"'I would have spoken of the importance of communication in marriage.'"

A poll found that ninety-seven percent of couples who rated their communication with their spouse as excellent considered themselves happily married, while among the couples who said their communication was poor, only fifty-six percent were happy with their marriage. The poll surmised "In an era of increasingly fragile marriages, a couple's ability to communicate is the single most important contributor to a stable and satisfying marriage."

When I was single, I had trouble understanding how communication could be difficult in marriage and why people made such a big fuss about it. I thought, how tough can this be? Just say what you mean, listen, and everything will be fine. I had no idea what I was talking about. Being in a close relationship with a woman on a day-to-day basis, I see much clearer what a daunting task communication can be. Men and women think and perceive things differently; they speak a different language and send different non-verbal signals. This seemingly simple task of sending and receiving messages is far more difficult than you might think.

Because good communication is so vital to a healthy marriage, you would be wise to begin mastering the art of communication during your single years.

Communication involves three basic elements: Perception, how we each uniquely see reality; Expression, how we try to share our point of view with others; and Understanding, how we try to make sense of the messages that the other person sends our way.

To avoid awkward use of pronouns as much as possible, I'll be using "Sara" and "Bob" in my examples of the way communication works. They are composite individuals and don't represent any one person. They are simply symbols of us all.

1. PERCEPTION.

Perception is the way things look from our individual point of view. As humans, we don't passively receive data like a disk being printed by a computer. When we receive data from our senses, we run it through a filter, selecting what we want, organizing, and interpreting it. The first problem between Sara and Bob and the rest of us, is that we each interpret reality through our own unique filter. We see life differently from each other!

Several factors make up a person's unique filter. Size, age, gender, skin color, and physical disabilities all affect the way we see life. For example, the house that I grew up in seems much smaller now that I am an adult; my change in height altered my perception. When Heidi is pregnant, she says it seems like there are so many more pregnant women around. Obviously the number of pregnant women has not changed. But the fact that Heidi has a protruding belly makes her more aware of women who are in a similar state. Likewise, a person in a wheelchair will take much more notice of ramps or the lack of them, whereas a fully-abled person wouldn't usually be aware of such things.

The culture you grow up in also affects the way things appear to you. The experience of butchering a pig or milking a cow will seem very different to a city slicker than it will to a farm boy. When we moved out to the country, I was squeamish about even taking raw meat out of the freezer. The first time I slit a chicken's rear end to pull out the guts, it took every ounce of raw masculine strength that I possessed just to keep the contents of my own stomach from coming out. Yet after a few years, the situation hardly fazed me.

Early on in our relationship, Heidi and I discovered just how much our past can affect our perception. Heidi came from a relatively small family (five kids) which was very proper, and in their household, interrupting someone else while they were talking was considered rude. I came from a big family where interrupting was vital if you wanted to be heard. When I was excited about the subject of conversation, I got my information out as fast as I could before the topic changed. So I would interrupt Heidi as a natural course of conversation and not think anything of it. But from her perspective, my interruption was a sign of disrespect and she was hurt by it. Thankfully, she opened up and shared this with me or I would have had no idea how my actions were coming across. After we talked it over, I was surprised to see how often I found myself interrupting.

One more example of how our past experiences color our perception: Heidi's sister Katrina committed suicide when Heidi was seventeen. Now she sometimes winces when someone casually throws out the expression, "I was killing myself laughing," whereas most of us wouldn't even notice it.

Another factor that makes our perception filter unique is how we physically feel in the moment. Headaches, nausea, and that sort of thing greatly affect the way we perceive sounds, smells, or just life in general. I am always surprised by how bleak and depressing the world seems when I'm sick, and how wonderful it is when my health returns. Our present feelings especially affect what we find funny; grief, tiredness, or agitation may make an otherwise funny joke seem just plain stupid. And of course, a feeling of being in love can make the world seem like a brighter, more inviting place.

In the course of married life, you will find how much your perception of your spouse and your marriage will be affected by mood swings and the natural ebb and flow of romantic feelings. During these early years of marriage, I've recognized my need to look at life from a broader perspective, and not let a current struggle or emotional issue distort the larger picture.

THE PROCESS OF PROCESSING

Not only do Sara and Bob have different filters receiving sensory data, but each of them also has a different way that they process the data, leading to even more differences in perception. Newspapers and journalists often "spin" the news by only sharing part of the facts and leaving out the other side of the story. So while the "facts" may be true, the overall picture may be distorted. Our minds can do the same thing by being selective in what we pay attention to and what we remember. We need to be aware that we may not always be getting an accurate picture.

WHAT WE MISS...

We're constantly being bombarded by smells, sounds, sights, etc.

If we absorbed all the data our senses give us, we would go crazy. It's as if we only have so much memory on the computer of our mind, so instead of crashing the computer, we're forced to be selective in what we absorb or ignore. I find it amazing how much we can see and hear and still miss. Because of this limitation we can end up with very distorted perceptions.

To illustrate this selectivity, let's say you're in a crowded room full of different ongoing conversations, when suddenly you hear your name spoken. Immediately you tune into that conversation. It's like your mind is scanning the available channels and decides what to dwell on. This tendency to tune in and tune out plays a huge role in our perception. When I am listening to a sermon or reading a book I often notice my mind wandering and time passes where I was "hearing" or "seeing" the words, but the message wasn't registering.

Our brain then goes on to retain only selective bits of what we randomly picked up and deletes the rest. Try this test: think about yesterday and what you remember about it, and you will find that there were certain things you heard or saw that you chose to remember and other things that were forgotten. What gets "saved" and "deleted" colors our perception. Past events can often seem more enjoyable or worse depending on what the mind chooses to retain. A hike up a mountain may be painful and grueling, but when you think about it a couple of days or weeks later, all you will remember is the thrill of conquering it and how good it felt to reach the base again. On the other hand, a bitter attitude can negatively color how past events are remembered. A grown man who harbors a grudge towards his father will be more likely to only remember the times his father was harsh or unfair and block out the times his father was kind or encouraging.

THE BLINDERS OF PREDETERMINED EXPECTATIONS

What our brain saves or deletes is influenced by our labeling and stereotyping of other people. We seem to need to put people in categories in our attempts to understand them. This can be helpful, but it often leads to destructive results when we label people unfairly, because we'll be more aware of the aspects of that person that fit our stereotype or label, and we may miss the things that contradict it. If we label someone as stingy or bossy, or grouchy, we'll tend to only see the things that reinforce this label. It's sobering to ponder just how much our labels cause us to presuppose certain things and affect our perception.

Heidi and I experienced this early in our marriage. Heidi is a terrific cook (one look at me will tell you that), and she told me she wanted to adjust her cooking to suit my tastes. After growing up in a family of eleven children where you didn't complain about the food – you just ate it – I salivated over this opportunity. So, meal after meal, I would tell her that the dish she'd fixed was awesome, and often offer an idea for how she could improve it so that it could be even more awesome next time. This went on for a few months. Looking back, it's hilarious how much disparity there was between our perceptions. From my perspective, I was an eat-anything-rave-about-everything husband who was clearly enjoying his wife's cooking, and I thought – compared to all the picky husbands out there – I must be such a joy to cook for. My self-imposed label influenced my selection of the data and how I saw our mealtime discussions.

Heidi filtered things differently – much differently. Her perspective finally came out in a teary post-midnight conversation. She told me that she saw me as a very picky eater and that she hardly ever felt that her food met my expectations and that she didn't like cooking for me as much as she used to. I was shocked! I couldn't believe what I was hearing! How much weight does a guy have to gain before he can shed the "picky" label? I told her how things looked from my angle, and reminded her that she was the one who told me she wanted to know exactly how I liked it. I also explained that I saw a picky eater as someone who refused to eat something – and I'd been faithfully eating everything served to me. I asked, "What about all the times that I told you the meal was perfect and I didn't offer any suggestions for improvement?" She countered with her perception and we were able to work things out.

I was so grateful she opened up, because I had no idea she felt that way. Once we looked at the situation from each other's perspective, we were able to shed our labels and see things more clearly. It turns out that my earlier comments and suggestions had hurt her, so she labeled me a picky eater and she started forming expectations based on that label, meaning she mainly remembered the times that I critiqued the meals. But, based on my label of myself, I looked at all the times I raved about the meals. It wasn't that one of us was seeing things that weren't there; we just weren't considering the balancing evidence because of our stereotyping. Since that time, I have tried to catch myself when I'm about to make suggestions, and try to wait for her to ask, and I also try to be more careful to praise her.

Heidi: It's working! Now that I know the difference between a connoisseur of food who knows how to make things taste better and someone who's just plain picky, I think Jesse's a total delight to cook for, because he really appreciates good food.

WHAT WE ADD...
Jesse: If leaving out part of the picture wasn't enough, we have an

ability to put things into the picture that aren't there. It's very hard for us to live with the unknown (or blank spaces). When Bob met Sara, she was like a picture covered with a grid of flaps, like an advent calendar. As Bob gets to know Sara better, more flaps are pulled back and he gets a bigger glimpse of who she is. However, the problem is that Bob only gets to pull back a few flaps at a time; much of Sara remains a mystery. Bob doesn't like the unknown, so he fills in the blanks and tricks himself into thinking he knows Sara better than he really does. Like the rest of us, Bob attempts to fill in the unknown in a couple of ways.

One, he assumes that people who are similar in one aspect will be similar in other ways as well. Oftentimes they will be, but not always. So if Bob already knows Sara's brother Jason and has just met Sara, he will assume that because both come from the same family they share similar convictions or personality traits. He may tend to read Jason's qualities into Sara. He may also group people together according to race, denomination, appearance, or physical build. Here's how it might work: Bob knows a few well-built, athletic guys, but he doesn't like the way these guys seem so arrogant and full of themselves. Because of this, when Bob meets Tim, who is muscular and athletic, even before Bob gets a chance to know him, he may assume that because Tim is similar in build to those other guys, he will also have the same annoying characteristics. But give Tim the benefit of the doubt! I happen to know from first-hand experience that it's possible to be athletic and have a great personality!

Secondly, Bob fills in the blanks by assuming that the way things are now is the way that they will stay. If he first meets Tim when he is terse or grouchy, he will assume that that is the way Tim always is and ignore the fact that he may have just been having a bad day. Or take for example people who are very quiet in large groups of people. It's easy to assume that these people are always quiet. But I've talked to family members of such people and have heard that some of them are really talkative clowns at home.

OBSERVATION VS. INTERPRETATION

After we make our observations about what people have done or said, we try to figure out why that person did this action. Sara can't observe motives, so all she can do is try to interpret why Bob did what he did. This becomes a problem when Sara fails to make a distinction between the facts (what she observed) and the interpretation (what she only guessed at). For example, Bob asks Sara how her brother Jason is doing in college. Sara observes Bob asking a question about Jason. But now she can interpret this question as either Bob being nosy or Bob showing love and care. If

Sara interprets the question as being nosy, she will go away thinking that she observed the nosiness, and won't even notice that she worked an interpretation in there.

I may observe Heidi being quiet or emotionally down and interpret that I have done something to offend her. It's important that I differentiate what I observed from what I interpreted. If I make a meal, I may observe Heidi eating quietly and not saying much about the food I fixed, and I'll interpret that she doesn't like it, or doesn't appreciate it. But maybe she is simply tired or has a lot on her mind. If I separate my interpretations from my observations, it frees me to ask Heidi to correct my interpretations rather than being hurt by what I "observed."

2. EXPRESSION.

Once we have formed our perception of reality, we then try to express these to each other. Unfortunately, none of us are mind readers so we are not able to simply swap thoughts for thoughts. To communicate her thoughts, Sara is forced to use words and gestures and attach meaning to them, hoping that Bob attaches the same meaning she did. If he attaches a different meaning, there has been a communication breakdown.

Let's look at some ways we humans express our thoughts and feelings and the difficulties that entail.

WHAT IS IN A WORD?

Scripture says that death and life are in the power of the tongue (Proverbs 18:21). We can bring life if we know how to use words well, but like a powerful piece of equipment, words can also cause great damage if we use them wrongly. Words can be a major obstacle to good communication because of the multiple meanings people attribute to them. Sara makes a huge mistake when she thinks that because she used a word a certain way Bob will use that word the same way.

My grandpa has a Ph. D. in linguistics and has translated much of the New Testament into the Blackfoot language. It's interesting to listen to him talk about the challenges of looking for Blackfoot equivalents that will communicate the same thought that the New Testament writer originally meant. If a translator is not careful, the message is often lost in translation. The phrase in English, "the flesh is weak but the spirit is willing", was translated by a computer into Russian and back into English, "the meat is bad but the wine is good." And then there was the Parisian who obviously had trouble while writing an English sign for his hotel, "Please leave your values at the front desk."

These difficulties seem obvious to us when translating other languages, but we forget that even when two people speak English they often still use the same English words in different ways. While words do have a dictionary meaning determined by majority consensus, they can change meaning. And words can mean something slightly different to other people because of connotation and past usage. In fact, I've read that the most common 500 English words have approximately 1400 different meanings; that means there's an average of almost three meanings per word! Consequently, it takes extra care and feedback to ensure that people are using your words the same way you are.

WELL, YOU KNOW...

We add complications when we speak in partial sentences, use sarcasm, humor, or allude to, but don't explicitly state something. You might think that words are pretty straightforward, but it's amazing how tone and inflection can alter the meaning, and obscure our message.

For example, the phrase "I love you" can be given several different meanings based on emphasis and voice inflection. If you state, "I love you?" with an upturned tone at the end, it seems to communicate: "You think I love you? Whatever gave you such a ridiculous idea?"

"I love you!" could mean: "I love you passionately!"

"I love you," delivered with a sarcastic downturn, could be sports trash talk, delivered either to a member of the opposite team who made a mistake that helped your team, or a sarcastic put down of an inept teammate.

Near the beginning of our relationship, Heidi was feeling overwhelmed by my overflow of verbal spray and this caused her emotions to temporarily short circuit. While I was constantly telling her I loved her, she couldn't bring herself to say "I love you" because she wasn't feeling it yet. One sunny day, we went with our families to an outdoor symphony concert. At the end of the day, I walked Heidi back to her parents' Suburban. Feeling madly in love, I was singeing her eyelashes with an intense gaze. I thought Heidi was feeling the love too, and as she reached her vehicle, she threw up her hands, exclaiming, "Okay, I'm in love!" I just sighed inside, "She love-loves me! I knew I would win her over."

I treasured that moment as the first time she told me she loved me. As it often happens, I had no idea how wrong I was. It wasn't till after we were married and we were reading my journal together that I discovered the truth. It turns out that Heidi was feeling very flustered by my intensity and was somewhat eager to leave and get some much needed space. She was so bent on getting out of there that she tripped on the curb. I didn't see this since the vehicle was between us. Jokingly referring to her absent-minded clumsiness, she sarcastically said, "Okay, I'm in love."

Oh well... she has since said "I love you" in many heartfelt ways and now I get the message correctly.

YOU SAY IT BEST WHEN YOU SAY NOTHING AT ALL...

To make matters worse for poor Sara and Bob, on top of their verbal language, they also send nonverbal messages through their facial expressions, gestures, and tone. But they each speak different body language. It is this way for everybody. Some people are generally quiet, some don't smile much, while others are flamboyant and very expressive. These differences make it very hard to interpret nonverbal language. We need to be sensitive to other people's background and past experience to recognize what nonverbal messages we may be sending and how they may be reading them.

Even something as simple as a smile can send many different messages. Take, for example, Bob who told his buddy, "Do you see that cute girl over there? She just smiled at me." His friend burst Bob's bubble by saying, "Oh, that's nothing. The first time I saw you I laughed out loud." It is amazing all that a smile can convey: mild disgust, affection, masked enthusiasm, excitement, humor, joy, nervousness, warmth, polite dismissal, etc. A smile can be hard to read even on the face of a spouse of many years.

In marriage, when you are much more tuned in to subliminal messages, things can get very complicated. The other day, we were getting ready to go to the city. I was eating my cold cereal in front of our laptop, getting my daily dose of Facebook and Blue Jays baseball news, when Heidi said with a sigh, "Okay, hon." Suddenly I was scratching my head, what does that mean? Is she saying, "Get off the computer and help me load the van!?" Or "I'm tired already, let's leave?" Or maybe, "I love you so much and I can't wait to get in the van with you!?" It's mind-boggling how much our tone can communicate...and not communicate!

IF YOU DON'T KNOW WHAT'S WRONG, I'M NOT GOING TO TELL YOU!

Besides the challenge of words having different meanings, we also face the question of how much each of us is willing to open up. Factors like pride or insecurity may prevent Bob from being completely open and honest about his feelings. Fear of embarrassment, ridicule, or criticism can lead Bob to either deliberate falsehood or silence. It might take a long time for Sara to earn Bob's trust before he will feel free to share what he is really feeling or thinking. Careless comments or ill-timed jokes could wound him deeply and make him very reluctant to open up.

If Bob's true feelings are not expressed, Sara will have no idea what Bob really feels, and rampant misunderstanding can spoil their relationship. Compounding the problem is the fact that Bob often expects people to know exactly what he is feeling regardless of the messages he is sending. But people can't read minds; they can only see behavior.

IT'S NOT WHAT YOU SAY, IT'S WHAT THEY HEARD

Sometimes people who are talkative and/or have a good command of the English language see themselves as much better communicators than they really are. Let's say Sara goes on an eloquent rant to Bob about how hard it is to find friends who really care about you and know how to be encouraging. She feels very satisfied afterward that she expressed what she felt. Great – but she already knew how she felt. The question is, did Bob accurately hear and interpret the message? Maybe Bob interprets Sara's message as a personal rebuke and feels terrible, or maybe he thinks Sara was referring to a mutual friend and wholeheartedly agrees with her analysis of the friend. Either way, what what was communicated, was only what Bob gets out of Sara's rant, whether that was what Sara meant or not.

Sara isn't a successful communicator until Bob rightly gets the message. This requires paying close attention to Bob's body language and frequently allowing him time for feedback. It doesn't matter how eloquent Sara is if Bob doesn't understand.

If a Russian came to you and gave a beautiful speech in his language, the eloquence factor means nothing if you didn't understand what he said. The only thing that gets communicated is what the other person interprets.

3. UNDERSTANDING.

This third aspect of the communication process is also fraught with potential for breakdown. Scripture realistically portrays the challenges related to communication and is full of exhortations about the importance of listening. Solomon writes that it is foolish to answer a matter before you have heard it (Proverbs 18:13), and James urges every man to be quick to hear and slow to speak (James 1:19). Diligence and care must be given if there is going to be successful communication, because, as you will see, accurately understanding and decoding the messages of others is no easy feat.

Sara wants to be known as a good listener, but unfortunately she isn't as good at it as she thinks she is. Listening is not just passive hearing, or just being quiet so the other person can talk. It's an active process by which we try to understand the other person. Dogs are good at being quiet and giving us an ear to vent our problems, but they are not successful listeners, because most of the time they don't have a clue what we are talking about. To be a good listener means that we can come to a correct understanding of the messages that others are sending. But several factors which can hinder good listening have to be overcome first.

WHAT FOREST? ALL I SEE IS THIS TREE

Sara tends to listen for details and facts instead of the main ideas or reasons why Bob is saying what he's saying. It's easy to squabble over little things and miss the fact that there could be agreement on the big things, such as when one person uses hyperbole to show their frustration and the other person takes it literally. For instance, a frustrated wife tells her husband that he is always late for dinner and the husband responds that such an accusation is not true because he was on time for a meal just last week.

Because of the different meanings words can have, we can be tripped up by the way a person uses a certain word and not hear the rest of their statement. When Heidi and I had our cooking/picky eater fiasco, we originally got hung up on the different ways we were using the word "picky."

Communication also often breaks down simply because the listener is using the same word in a different way than the speaker used it. Sara and Bob have argued vehemently about whether dating is an acceptable practice for Christians. They actually agree with each other, but are using the loaded term dating in different ways. Sara thinks dating is fine because she uses the word dating to mean casual get-togethers with friends. Bob thinks dating is wrong because to him dating means carefree, uncommitted romance. It is important to seek to understand what the other person means by their particular use of the word.

Such disagreements often occur in debates over doctrine. Terms such as free will, Calvinism, Arminianism, and election become emotionally charged words that people fight over without first seeking to understand what the other person means by these terms. If someone says to you, "I don't believe we have free will," seek to understand what he means by free will, instead of just reacting to him. You may actually agree. It is a good habit to ask what the other person means by a certain phrase, or even better, to ask, "This is what I hear you saying when you use this word. Am I correct? Or do you mean something else?"

SORRY, I WAS DISTRACTED

On top of the complex problems of interpreting what she hears, sometimes Sara misses what Bob says because of distractions. The message can be lost simply because of loud noise or physical exhaustion. While physical distractions can prevent Sara and Bob from getting the whole message, I believe mental distractions are the biggest factors that prevent understanding. We seem to have a lot of trouble focusing on what others are really saying.

Sometimes the reason for this is pride – I think I know Heidi better than I really do. This can lead me to assume I know what Heidi is going to say and then I don't genuinely listen to her. Or sometimes I convince myself that I have psychic powers and can discern what Heidi is really trying to say, and then I read a subliminal message into her statement. Either way, I don't honor Heidi if I don't truly focus on what she is saying. I say this from experience: Don't jump to conclusions!

Other times I miss what people are saying because I am insecure in some area and this makes me defensive. Because I spend more energy trying to defend myself or my point of view, I don't listen well. During the time when I should be listening, I'm formulating a response or a comeback. I've been involved in conversations peppered with needless contention. Even when there was ultimately agreement, a defensive spirit got us jumping to defend ourselves rather than stepping back and trying to understand what the other person was really saying. An example of this is when someone is explaining a point of view, and because of my defensiveness I wrongly interpret his words as a personal attack and I interrupt him to defend myself rather than letting him finish.

Bob and Sara have sensitive points based on past hurts, such as their appearance, weight, accomplishments, and deeply held views. They are very protective of these areas that have been ridiculed or challenged in the past. When topics related to their sensitive spots come up, Bob and Sara throw up defenses. When Bob is in self-defense mode, he finds it hard to really listen to what Sara is saying. It's easy for him to assume that when Sara broaches the subject of his accomplishments, for example, she is attempting to hurt him. It's as if Bob has posted sentries around this area who become paranoid and see an enemy behind every bush. Apparently, Bob thinks it's safer to suspect an enemy where there isn't one than to be caught off guard by an enemy from an unexpected source. But jumpy soldiers often accidentally shoot the allies.

There is great wisdom in being "quick to hear and slow to speak" (James 1:19). If you feel yourself becoming defensive, slow down, bite your tongue, let the other person finish, and ask clarifying questions before you shoot back a reply or assume ill intent on the part of the person who is speaking to you.

COMMUNICATION IS **DIFFICULT**

As you can see, communication is an extreme challenge even under the best of circumstances. In a basic two-way exchange, there are at least six possible points for a breakdown in communication or a misunderstanding of reality in a relationship.

1. Sara's perception of reality.
2. Sara attempts to put her thoughts into words.
3. What Bob hears.
4. How Bob interprets the message.
5. Bob attempts to put his thoughts into words.
6. What Sara hears.

When Sara begins to interpret the return message, her perception will affect her understanding and the process will begin again. At each of these points, there is real potential for communication breakdown and misunderstanding.

A Finnish researcher named Osmo Wiio summed up the problems of communication by writing "Wiio's Laws of Communication." Similar to "Murphy's Laws," these are pessimistic and somewhat tongue-in-cheek, but they are sadly accurate.

WIIO'S LAWS OF COMMUNICATION

1. Communication usually fails, except by accident.

   a. If communication can fail, it will.

   b. If communication cannot fail, it still most usually fails.

   c. If communication seems to succeed in the intended way, there's a misunderstanding.

   d. If you are content with your message, communication certainly fails

2. If a message can be interpreted in several ways, it will be interpreted in a manner that maximizes the damage.

3. There is always someone who knows better than you what you meant with your message.

4. The more we communicate, the worse communication succeeds.

   a. The more we communicate, the faster misunderstandings propagate.

5. In mass communication, the important thing is not how things are but how they seem to be.

6. The more important the situation is, the more probably you forget an essential thing that you remembered a moment ago.

The more realistic your picture of the difficulty of communication is, the better your chances are of communicating successfully. When you expect it to be easy, you won't take the necessary measures that are vital to good communication.

WAYS TO OVERCOME THE CHALLENGES OF COMMUNICATION

Communication provides some of the most difficult challenges we humans have to face. Thankfully, our Owner's manual, the Bible, contains the remedy for poor communication. It is found in Philippians 2:1-5: "If you have any encouragement from being united with Christ, if any comfort from His love, if any fellowship with the Spirit, if any tenderness and compassion, then make my joy complete by being like-minded, having the same love, being one in spirit and purpose. Do nothing out of selfish ambition or vain conceit, but in humility consider others better than yourselves. Each of you should look not only to your own interests, but also to the interests of others."(NIV)

The key to successful communication is in seeking to understand rather than being understood. As long as you have two people trying to get their point across, neither will accurately hear what the other is saying. But the moment both people seek first to understand and really listen, communication will flow. Good communication is not merely about skills; it is about love and humility.

DEALING WITH PROBLEMS OF PERCEPTION

"In humility, consider others better than yourselves."

We need to realize that we can be wrong in our assessment of a situation. It's crucial that we learn to question the way things appear to us. An unquestioning trust in our ability to perceive reality leaves us wide open to error. Simply recognizing that first impressions can be very misleading, and that there is much more to a situation than first meets the eye, will greatly increase our chances of accurately perceiving situations.

- Acknowledge the limitations of perception.

If you realize how limited your own perspective is, you will see the need to ask others how things look to them. Rather than accusing others of being dishonest or wrong, recognize that things simply looked different from their vantage point. Learn to appreciate their point of view instead of writing it off.

- Differentiate between observation and interpretation

If you want successful relationships, you'll have to learn to make a distinction between observation and inferences and not jump to conclusions. Ask, "Was this an observation or inference?" If it was inference, look for multiple interpretations; the law of love requires us to give others the benefit of the doubt. Verify your own inferences by asking those involved if your interpretation was correct instead of simply assuming that it was.

- Try not to label or stereotype people, but instead reserve judgment.

Again, when you are tempted to categorize someone in a negative way, ask if this is accurate and if there is perhaps some balancing evidence. Ask yourself if you are wrongly assuming negative things about someone because of a similarity to someone else.

- Look for the good in people.

Remember, we see what we want to see – it's the way perception works. If you want to only see the negative side of a person, then that is all you will see. Look for things to affirm in people and the change in how you perceive others will be dramatic.

DEALING WITH PROBLEMS OF EXPRESSION
"Do nothing out of selfish ambition or vain conceit."

When you talk, it should be for the benefit of others. If you speak with the other person in mind, your ability to communicate will be greatly improved. Here are some ways to do this.

- Shape the message for the listener.

Try to keep in mind how your words may be coming across. How are the other person's perception filters, such as his past experience or current feelings, affecting his interpretation? Adjust your message accordingly. For instance, if you know a person is struggling with feeling overweight, drop any fat jokes.

Remember that you already know what you think and feel, so you are expressing your thoughts for the benefit of the other person. Don't lose sight of the fact that what the other person received and interpreted is the only thing that was communicated. Don't blame the other person for misunderstanding; it is your job to try to make sure you spoke in a way that enabled them to understand what you were saying.

- Stop and ask for feedback to be sure the message is being interpreted accurately.

Take time to ask, "What do you think? Do you agree? What did you hear me say? What did the situation look like from your perspective?"

- Use "I" statements instead of "you" statements.

If I could impart just one piece of marriage advice, it would be this simple principle that has helped Heidi's and my communication more than just about anything else: Use statements acknowledging that what you are saying is simply your perception of what is happening and that you could be wrong. When you say, "This is what I heard," or "I feel like this," or "This is how it looked to me," you enable the other person to listen without becoming defensive.

In contrast, when you make accusatory statements that begin with "you said" or "you did," you can put that person on the defensive, and make it very difficult for them to hear what you're saying. A simple change of phrasing can have a huge effect. When Heidi and I were discussing my critiques of her cooking, if she had said, "You are so picky," I would have gotten defensive and tried to prove that I wasn't. However, because she phrased it, "I feel like you are picky," I couldn't argue with her perception and I was forced to check into what was making her feel that way, instead of merely justifying myself. (**Heidi**: Good for me, huh? I'm a quick learner.)

- Avoid statements like "always" and "never."

These cause the listener to get hung up on details and miss what you're trying to say. We sometimes resort to hyperbole (exaggeration used for emphasis or effect) to make a point, but often understatement is more effective in getting through to the other person. Again, make sure to phrase your frustrations with the other person in a way that acknowledges that this is simply your perception, rather than a statement of fact.

- Say what you mean.

Take care that you're saying what you really mean. If you become careless in what you're expressing, you can hopelessly confuse your listener. It is risky to open up and be honest about what you're thinking and feeling, but it is the only way other people can know how you truly feel. Don't blame others for not knowing about your sore spots. People aren't mind readers; they can only see behavior and hear what you say. It's not the fault of others if you haven't honestly communicated your true feelings.

- Be aware of semantic differences.

In other words, be mindful of the variation in meaning that words can have. Try to get into the habit of saying things like, "This is what I mean when I use this word."

- Be aware of the nonverbal signals you may be sending.

Make sure your body language communicates what your mouth is saying and is not sending a contradictory message. Your tone of voice and facial gestures may be sending a message of their own!

DEALING WITH PROBLEMS OF UNDERSTANDING

"Each of you should look not only to his own interests but also the interests of others."

- Give your undivided attention.

Really focus on the other person. Don't start formulating a response while you're listening. This can be tough sometimes, I know. If you miss something, make sure you ask them to repeat it. It can be very dangerous to try and guess what the person said, or to try piecing it together from what you did hear. The other night Heidi and I were cuddling and she told me sweetly, "I don't feel whole when I'm with others and you're not there." What I heard was, "I don't feel a hole when you're not there." I thought, "That's nice, honey, why are you bringing that up now?" But we got it straightened out... I think.

- Don't assume you know what they are going to say.

Be careful that your stereotyping or labeling of a person does not affect what you hear or don't hear. Try not to complete other people's sentences. I laugh as I write that, because it is a huge weakness of mine. I do it to try and show that I am tracking with them, but I think they would be better served if I just bit my tongue and let them find the right words and finish the sentences on their own.

- Give descriptive feedback.

This point is vital. Learn to ask questions like, "This is what I heard you say. Am I right? Is this what you meant?" Try to repeat back in your own words what you heard and then give the other person a chance to clarify. Don't just parrot what was said; it is important that you paraphrase using new words, otherwise you may be using the same words in different ways and neither of you will know it.

- Give the speaker a safe place to open up.

As you listen, be very careful not to ridicule what the person is saying and don't be too quick to correct them, either. If the other person doesn't feel safe, they won't open up and fully express what they're feeling or thinking. It can take a long time to earn a person's trust and a careless comment or joke can do a lot of damage. Try to hold your tongue if you feel like judging a person's point of view or criticizing them for feeling a certain way. There is a time for loving rebuke and correction, but a person needs to feel safe before they will venture to be honest and open.

This was a lesson I had to learn to get Heidi to open up about her feelings. In my family, we liked to have everything out in the open, so we were very vocal about what bothered us and we'd make it clear to each other when we were offended. This, of course, has led to some epic thunderstorms of emotion, but we always apologized and the air was clear again. The sweetest smell is right after a rain storm. Heidi, on the other hand, was used to internalizing her displeasure and negative emotions. The way she wanted to deal with conflict was to get some space and work through it alone. At first I was unprepared for this. I wanted to talk everything over and she wanted silence and space. I could have handled yelling and physical abuse (wrestling Heidi is fun!), but I didn't know how to deal with silence.

So, to help her open up, I had to be patient and very gentle. She told me she was hesitant to share what she was feeling for fear that I would criticize her or think what she was feeling was foolish. I had to earn her trust by proving that I was a safe place to be open. It's something I still have to be careful about. When Heidi shares her fears and struggles, I'm tempted to be quick with advice and exhortations. But most of the time that's not what she needs. She already knows what I am going to say anyway. She just needs to know that I care about what she is feeling and that I can listen without being too quick to try fixing her problems.

- Listen for why a person may be saying something.

It is such a valuable exercise to put yourself in the other person's shoes and seek to look at life from their perspective. When you listen, try to be sensitive and tuned into the emotions behind the words. If a person is expressing anger or frustration, don't get caught up in the details of what he is saying, rather, seek to understand. Try to put yourself in his shoes and consider the different factors that are affecting his perception. However, do not assume too much. Once you have tried to get inside their mind, make sure to ask if you have an accurate perception.

COMMUNICATION IS WORTH THE WORK

It's deeply satisfying to be in close relationships with other people. When you boil things down, you discover that good relationships mean far more than money, fame, or power. But these relationships depend upon an ability to communicate, which takes a lot of work. I have tailored much of this chapter to the challenges involved in marriage communication, but hopefully you can apply these points to your current relationships. Serve those around you by carefully developing your communication skills. Ask God to give you a gentle tongue and a sensitive, understanding ear, and then go tell someone you love them and make sure it gets communicated properly!

CHAPTER 10

ESCAPE THE DEVASTATION OF LUST

He had received strict instructions, "No matter what happens, do not touch or smell any of the flowers along the road. They are lethal – extremely poisonous!"

As he walked toward the perilous path, he remembered yawning at the desperate tone with which the old man gave the warning. What could be so dangerous about flowers? After all, how hard could it be to avoid touching or smelling flowers? His mind soon wandered to other things.

The young man started down the road and soon noticed the flowers. These were not ordinary flowers. They had color more rich and brilliant than anything he had ever seen, and the texture of the petals looked like smooth velvet. Their fragrance sent a delicious sensation through his whole body. Intense craving flooded him. He ached to pluck a flower and breathe deeply of its tantalizing aroma.

The urgent warning came back to him, but it was quickly consumed by the flaming fire of his desire. He had to have one of the flowers. His legs went weak at the sight of them all. With trembling hands, he reached for a rose-like beauty. His fingers wrapped around the stem – what a delightful feel it had on his skin! It came out of the ground effortlessly, as if it wanted to be held. He lifted it to his face and inhaled deeply.

In a moment, the fragrant aroma became a hideous stench, the blissful sensation that had been caressing his body flared into a flesh-eating fire. But worse still was the anguish of soul, the inner turmoil that began to eat at him. In agony he crumpled to the ground, lying there for hours as the poison slowly sucked every last bit of life from his tormented body.

In fairy tales, we are warned against plants, fruits, and potions. In real life, we are warned against lust. Nothing has the ability like lust does to make something so destructive look so appealing and to make some so beautiful so damaging. When raging desire has been let loose outside the safe, secure confines of marriage, lethal poison appears inviting. The very thing that will kill your chances of finding satisfaction, ruin your prospects of a happy marriage, and possibly even take your own life (Proverbs 7), looks like a harmless piece of candy that you just have to have. Lust is one of the greatest saboteurs of marriages today.

The pull of your God-given desires for physical affection and sex are so strong that if you do not submit them to the authority of Christ – i.e., only feeding these desires within a marriage relationship – they will turn into lust and make you their slave. You'll eventually become so consumed by them that you will always crave and never be satisfied. But unlike the story above, where the consequences were immediate, in reality, it may take years before you reap the bitter fruit of your wrong choices.

God's Word is full of repeated warnings about how devastating lust is. We are told to flee, no questions asked. In the heat of the moment, just run, don't reason, or you will lose.

There are several truths that will guard your mind and put lust into perspective. At the first stage of temptation, a review of these principles can douse the little spark before it bursts into a wild fire. I have found some biblical ways to keep you from the immoral woman (or, for you girls, the immoral man – he's definitely out there!), and consequently, from death itself. I have made them easier to remember by using the acronym E-S-C-A-P-E. For some of the letters, I have attached more than one "battle strategy." In order to better remember the acronym, just pick the strategy for each letter that is most helpful to you. These are time-tested and well-worn truths in my life. I know what a terrible struggle fighting lust involves. These truths were lifelines in my fight against sexual temptation.

If you want to prepare for a successful marriage, it's so important that you learn to conquer lust. I pray that these steps will enable you do to that. For you girls, I'm directing this mainly to guys, but much of it is very applicable to you, too. Please keep reading!

E-Eternal perspective

In the face of temptation, we usually only think about what we want right now, and we give little thought to long-term consequences. Stepping out of the now to take a look at your life from the bigger perspective of eternity will show lust for what it is – a destroyer of all that is beautiful. Think of the cost of a temporary thrill: guilt, shame, enslavement, and eventually, causing a sense of betrayal and insecurity in the very one that you want to protect and cherish.

Someday you may fall in love with a beautiful woman. You're going to feel an incredibly strong desire to protect and cherish her. The thought of seeing her in pain will be a thought that brings great anguish. When you take her in your arms, are you going to know with confidence that you are a safe place for her? Or are you going to be her source of pain? When a wife knows that her husband is looking elsewhere for satisfaction, it's a terrible blow to her sense of worth. A wife longs for the assurance that she is all the beauty her husband needs to be satisfied. Every time your wife sees you looking where you shouldn't or discovers your lust addictions, the effect will be like a knife plunged into the very heart that you would do anything to protect.

The consequences of this pain can be devastating for you. Do you think she will feel like being intimate with a man who is cheating mentally on her? Knowing your head is filled with airbrushed, unrealistic women will make her feel terribly unbeautiful. A wife needs to feel beautiful before she can have a desire to give herself to her husband. I can't say this strongly enough – giving into lust will never satisfy! It is like drinking salt water when you are thirsty. The more you drink, the more you want.

But do you know what does satisfy? True intimacy with a real woman. I'm not just talking about sex, but the emotional closeness that comes from romance – soul intimacy. The stereotype is that guys want sex and women want romance. I disagree. Like I mentioned in a previous chapter, what really satisfies me is the romantic aspect of life: The long walks at sunset, the candlelit dinners, the heart to heart late night conversations, and the way Heidi looks at me after I've served her in some way. In my relationship with Heidi, I feel satisfied at every level! Lust can give temporary relief to a biological function, but it will leave you feeling more and more empty, both spiritually and emotionally. Guys need emotional and spiritual closeness to be satisfied. Lust destroys your chances of finding either.

In contrast, it is more satisfying than you can imagine to have a good marital relationship, a wife who trusts you, and a clear conscience before God. When you bring your sex drive under the authority of Christ, it can be a wonderful thing. Let your need for physical intimacy be something that drives you towards your wife, not something that pushes you apart. Deal lust a blow by learning to think long-term.

S-SACRIFICE YOUR BODY, STARVE YOUR SEX DRIVE, SET YOURSELF UP FOR SUCCESS

Sacrifice your body – Paul instructs us to present our bodies as a living sacrifice to God. Christ paid an immeasurable price to redeem you, giving His life for you so that you might be saved. To receive this gift you must give your life to Christ. He must be Lord of your entire life, not just your actions, but also your thoughts. In God's eyes, lustful thoughts are just as wrong as lustful actions: "But I tell you that anyone who looks at a woman lustfully has already committed adultery with her in his heart" (Matthew 5:28 NIV). No matter how many times you have failed, you still have the obligation to your Savior to surrender yourself to Him. He gave His all so that you could be free. You also need to give Him your all so that you can be free.

If you rebel against Christ's authority over your life, the result will not be freedom but enslavement to a vile enemy. You have one of two choices: Either to be enslaved to the one who hates you and wants you destroyed, or to surrender your life to your Creator, a kind and gentle Master who loves you more than life itself, and only wants what's best for you.

Starve your sex drive – Many guys feel like they have a sex drive that's just too strong to handle. What they don't realize is that lustful thoughts and visual stimuli such as pornography will grow the sex drive way beyond what God intended it to be. If you stop feeding your lust, your sex drive will shrink back to a more manageable strength. But you will have to be patient; it will take a while. I have read though, that if you can starve yourself from any sexual stimuli for just three weeks, you'll find it much easier to fight temptation after that. Your body will have adjusted, and you can be a man with self-control.

Set yourself up for success - My brother-in-law, Andy, was a resident director at Cedarville University, overseeing and giving counsel to a dorm of male students for three years. He had some very helpful advice for men who struggled with pornography. He used an illustration from the movie "Gettysburg." In the movie, there was a battle where the North had the high ground and the South was forced to attack running uphill through an open field. The South faced heavy losses because they were fighting from a position of weakness; they had no covering and were being mowed down. Andy's point was that you need a strategy that will help you succeed. You need to stay away from situations that will make defeat inevitable. So if your problem is pornography when you are alone with the computer, try to put your computer in a place where others can see you. Or get some software that will email to your accountability partner a list of the websites you visited. If there are certain times and places you always find yourself losing, identify them and see what you can do to find greater protection during your weak moments.

C-CRUCIFY YOUR FLESH, COVENANT NOT TO LUST, CLEANSE YOUR HOUSE, CONTROL YOUR MIND

Crucify your flesh – Paul instructs you to "count yourself dead to sin" (Romans 6:11 NIV). When you make Christ your Lord, you're identifying yourselves with His death. You've died with Him so that you may truly live with Him. It is helpful during temptation to visualize yourself as a corpse. A corpse is completely unresponsive to the lures of sin. We should have the same attitude toward the things that will destroy us.

Covenant not to lust – Make a covenant with your eyes to not lust after any woman you are not married to (Job 31:1). When you're tempted, remember that your eyes belong to God, and that you have no right to look lustfully at someone who does not belong to you. This is vital to a healthy marriage. Looking at a woman in a way that starts your engines is a form of foreplay. Your wife is the only person you should be looking at that way. I'm sure you think it would be wrong to just go up to a woman and fondle or kiss her, because your wife would feel betrayed. Looking lustfully is being unfaithful to your wife, and you will pay the consequences. You have no right to look that way at a woman any more than you have the right to kiss or fondle her. She belongs to another man. If you are looking, you're stealing from another man, and also giving away something that belongs to your wife. When you marry, your eyes belong to your wife alone. If you're not yet married, they should still belong to her, even if you have never met her. Faithful eyes are one of the most precious and romantic gifts that you can give a woman. (**Heidi:** Absolutely - amen!!)

There is a difference between seeing a woman and looking lustfully at her. You can't help it when a scantily clad woman walks by, but you can control your eyes. If you find yourself receiving sexual pleasure from looking at a woman, it is time you looked away. However, it's so much easier if you can learn to bounce your eyes even before you get turned on. Train yourself to look away immediately, before the image gets a chance to register. Guarding your eyes also includes guarding your mind. When an image is flashed before your eyes, you have the responsibility to choose to discard that image rather than ponder it for a while. Remembering that I have made a covenant to not look lustfully at any other woman has often stopped me from getting careless with my eyes and looking a little too long.

Heidi: Guys, I know it's unbelievably tough to do daily battle against the visual temptations from magazines, movies, internet, and women in your church, school, or workplace. And when you see guys you respect with lust in their eyes, looking twice at immodesty, it's even harder to keep your guard up. It makes you wonder, "Who isn't looking?" But please, please keep on fighting every day with God's strength to resist the temptations to look and lust. You answer to God for your purity, not for the fallen standards of men around you, or the motives of the immodest women who make your life difficult. You have a precious woman out there, somewhere, waiting for you. And she longs for a Prince Charming who will honestly tell her she's the one and only most beautiful woman he has ever laid eyes on. Do you know how much security I find in knowing that Jesse loves me passionately without comparing me to any other woman? I trust him and freely love him because, ever since he was a small boy, he's worked at guarding his eyes. With me, he has nothing to hide. He's not going somewhere else for satisfaction. I *love* knowing that he's completely mine and I am completely his.

Cleanse your home –

Jesse: This is one of the most practical and effective ways to escape lust...Cleanse your home! It will be so much easier if you don't keep things around that will cause you to stumble. As a teen, I often felt like a raging fire. I'm so glad that we had a cleansed home because there were frequent times where I don't think I would have had the strength to not look at something I shouldn't have.

Talk to your mom and sisters. I'll bet they would be happy to help you. My sister Emily would tear out pages or scribble over inappropriate images. Mom made sure that magazines and catalogs were thrown away or had the offensive ads torn out. Mom or Emily would preview movies or check them out at www.kids-in-mind.com or www.pluggedin.com, so we would know which parts to fast-forward if we watched the movies at all, and our little sisters, Amy and Hannah, would often find a pillow or a book to cover up any immodesty on the TV screen. These precautions made it so much easier for us boys growing up. This is a simple strategy but it will make a world of difference!

Control your mind – Conquering lust starts with controlling your mind. This was the area in which I struggled most as a single man. The mind is the easiest place to give into lust – it's quick and it's private. Because of this, it is also the hardest place to find victory. But whether you find success or defeat in dealing with sexual temptation will depend on whether you win the battle in the mind. There are a few things that helped me in this area.

The first one is to realize your mind is not private; God sees it and you will give an account to Him of your thought life. If you are not sure if a thought is pure or not, try this experiment: Imagine your mind as a theater and what you choose to think about is on display for others to see. How would your future wife feel sitting in the front row? What about if your mom and sisters saw it – would you be ashamed?

A second way is to replace the lewd images with counter images. It doesn't work to not think about something. For example, don't think about white elephants. What did you just think about? The way to not think about white elephants is to think about something else. When you are tempted by a lustful fantasy, picture your wife in tears, hurt by your betrayal. Picture Jesus' body bloodied and broken beyond recognition to pay for your sins. Or picture the joy of standing before your wife with a clear conscience and telling her that you have fought valiantly for her and you're not going to stop fighting to maintain your purity.

A third way is to memorize and meditate on Scripture. This is discussed in the next letter of our battle strategy acronym. Even if the scripture you are meditating on doesn't have anything to do with defeating lust, it will still give your mind a healthy alternative to the poison you think you want.

Finally, be careful what you feed your mind. Our mind has to process what goes in. If you are filling your mind with graphic descriptions of immorality, or lewd portrayals of lust, you will find that the battle in your thought life will be far more difficult. One of my weaknesses was reading graphic descriptions in novels or even marriage manuals. I would get a rush even thinking about flipping through a book in search of tantalizing word pictures. However, when I actually did find something graphic, my rush of excitement was immediately replaced by overwhelming guilt and a sense of defilement. I knew that I had another painful confession to make or I would not be free. I am so grateful for the purifying effect guilt had on me, because it kept me from further defiling my mind. As it was, the images those words created caused enough trouble and would haunt me when I was trying to go to sleep or had too much free time to think.

A-APPLY THE WARNINGS OF SCRIPTURE AND ACCOUNTABILITY

Apply the warnings of Scripture – The book of Proverbs uses strong and graphic language when warning about sexual temptation from "the immoral woman." The immoral woman is not just the prostitute, but any woman, real or imagined, who tempts you to lust after her body, causing you to be unfaithful to your spouse. Proverbs 5-7 especially deal firmly with this. The immoral woman is described as having "lips that drip honey," but her "house leads straight to the grave." We are told not to stray near her path or be allured by her beauty, because we will pay a huge price for it, now or later.

A verse I often kept close by was James 1:16-17, "Do not be deceived, my beloved brethren. Every good gift and every perfect gift is from above, and comes down from the Father of lights, with whom there is no variation or shadow of turning." This verse reminded me that God was the only one who could offer real satisfaction. To think otherwise was a deception that would bring ruin.

Commit to memory several of these warnings, and use them as buckets of cold water to douse the fiery darts of lust.

Accountability – It is almost impossible to defeat sexual sin such as pornography or masturbation while you are keeping it a secret. You need to confess these sins to a brother in Christ and ask him to keep you accountable. Knowing that you will have to report your failure will cause you to think twice about indulging in sin. I had a friend who told me that he was struggling to overcome a certain sin, and we set a weekly check-up time. He said that knowing he was going to be asked about this sin was not only a major deterrent to giving into it, but also a real help in finding victory. Make sure you find someone you respect who will hold you accountable. If you find someone who simply says, "It's okay, we all struggle with it," he's not going to be much help. Yes, we all battle temptation to sexual sin, but victory can be found. It's important that your accountability partner recognizes that.

P-PERCEIVE WOMEN THE WAY JESUS WOULD

Women are often portrayed as objects for men's gratification. When Jesus walked this earth, prostitutes were so strongly drawn to Him. I believe that they saw in His eyes a genuine love for who they really were – thinking, feeling humans. Up to this point, they had either been looked at with lust and felt like objects, or with disdain and disgust, and felt like trash. Jesus saw them as women made in the image of God, hungry for love and acceptance – women who hurt deeply and longed to be cherished and protected. When you are tempted to lust after a woman's body, remember her soul and ask, "How would Jesus see her?"

Learn to view a woman as someone else's daughter. Think about how you would want men to look at your own precious little girl. How would you feel if you saw a man leering after your daughter? This may not be that effective until you have a little girl of your own. But once you have held the little angel in your arms and have vowed to do anything to protect her, you will understand.

When a woman puts her body on display and is trying to sell herself, it is a sign of deep neediness. I grieve for these women because they are buying into the lie that their worth is based on their measurements and sex appeal. But no woman can hope to live a normal life and keep that shape. Based on that standard, she will soon feel empty and worthless, which is sad, because a woman has much more value than her worth as a sex object. No matter her age or shape, a woman still has so much to offer the world. When God created the world, He saved the best for last. Women are God's precious handiwork, the jewel of creation. Learn to see them as God does and don't demean them with a lustful stare.

E-ENJOY GOD AND HIS WAYS

It is not enough to focus on what we must avoid. We must be proactive in enjoying the good gifts that God gave us! Our deepest longing is not sexual release but intimacy with God. If that longing is not fulfilled, nothing else will satisfy. If we are filled with God, we will find the grace to enjoy life regardless of what He asks of us. God's laws are for our benefit! He would not ask us to keep sex within marriage if this was not the best way to enjoy the gift. Thank God for your desires in this area and look forward to His fulfillment of them.

Physical intimacy is one of God's greatest gifts, intended to cement the marriage covenant and draw a husband and wife together. But God's purposes for sex are not merely to give pleasurable sensations to your skin. If you make sex a selfish pursuit of pleasure, you will find that the sensations are wonderful but fleeting and only make you feel emptier. This is because the purpose of sex is to create intimacy with another person, to experience the joy of full self-disclosure and of knowing the other person totally and completely.

Sex is supposed to be something that pulls us out of ourselves and trains our eyes on the other. Pornography and masturbation turn sex into a selfish pursuit that keeps us enslaved within ourselves. C.S. Lewis had this to say about self stimulation, "For me, the real evil of masturbation would be that it takes an appetite which, in lawful use, leads an individual out of himself to complete (and correct) his own personality in that of another (and finally in children and grandchildren) and turns it back, sends the man back into the prison of himself, there to keep a harem of imaginary brides. And his harem, once admitted, works against his ever getting out and really uniting with a real woman."

Sex is satisfying only when it is an expression of love and sacrificial giving. God created sex to be a reflection of the kind of intimacy He wants to enjoy with us. He is passionate about making sure this gift fulfills its function. He knows that sexual perversion will keep you from being able to enjoy Him. He also knows that the only thing that will give you the motivation and desire to overcome sexual immorality is to enjoy a relationship with Him. Surrender to God your desires for love and physical intimacy. Find your satisfaction in Him.

A WOMAN'S PERSPECTIVE ON DEALING WITH LUST

Heidi: Now to you girls…much of what Jesse said above was directed to young men, but women struggle with lust too, just in different ways. I want to look at a couple of areas I struggled with as a young single woman – areas that may be common problems for some of you girls and women.

My sister Katrina committed suicide at college when she was nineteen. In her suicide letter to us, she said she was tired of struggling to win her battle with bulimia, a battle my family and I had been trying to help her fight victoriously. But the next part of her letter shocked us; she said she had begun viewing pornography online. While she was drawn back to it again and again, she also hated it, felt ashamed, and wanted to escape its filthy clutches. So she chose death.

Pornography is primarily a problem unique to men. They tend to have a stronger sex drive and need for sexual release, and are generally more visually stimulated than women. However, there are a lot of women who are addicted to pornography. According to one review, one of three visitors to all adult websites are women, and 9.4 million women access adult websites every month. The website, www.freedombeginshere.org cites a ChristiaNet.com survey which found that "50% of Christian guys and 20% of Christian girls struggl[e] with pornography."

How did Katrina start into pornography? She was a good Christian girl, very modest, proper and reserved toward guys, and brought up in a home where movies and books were carefully screened to guard against inappropriate content of any kind. Before Katrina left for college, she and I had a late-night talk about struggling with our thoughts and temptations to focus on sexual things. It was the only time we ever opened up and shared on the subject. Both of us were kind of relieved to find out that we weren't alone in our battle against occasionally thinking about guys in an inappropriate way, letting our minds wander with curiosity in a direction we weren't supposed to go yet. We knew it was wrong to fantasize about guys and their bodies, to lust, to imagine what physical intimacy was like. We always felt dirty and guilty afterward. But what to do when such thoughts just randomly popped into our minds? They were so powerful, and oftentimes, before we knew it, we were off on a mental path headed toward frustration. Thankfully, because we were so protected and naïve, we didn't really have much of anything to imagine.

But in the months just before her suicide, Katrina gave into temptation and began to fill her mind with pornographic images that fed her fantasies. Now she had explicit things running through her imagination. And she felt dirtier and guiltier than ever. In a paper we found after her death, Katrina had written that she hated how this new awareness made her feel awkward around other people; she could no longer think of others in a normal, healthy way. She'd allowed herself to become more vulnerable to lust and fantasies.

If you find yourself with such unbidden thoughts like these, you have my total understanding and sympathy. I wish Katrina and I had talked more. We could have held each other accountable, praying for one another and asking often, "How's your thought life? What can I do to help you be pure?" Instead, we each went on to battle alone. Katrina lost. I still ache for her, and deeply regret that she was never able to experience the pure, soaring joy of love and intimacy the way I have. By God's grace, I didn't go down the path Katrina did. It helped so much not to have actual specific pictures littering my mind. I fought hard against the occasional temptation to lust, and cried out to God to help me. I needed His strength many times through my single years.

Was there a way Katrina could have regained ground – habits she could have formed to protect against the onslaught of tempting thoughts? Absolutely!

Jesse shared earlier some really helpful suggestions for fighting the war against lust. I hope you will use them to begin finding victory. I don't believe you are responsible for the thoughts that pop into your mind, but you're definitely responsible for how you respond to them. If you're tempted to lust or fantasize about guys or look at pornography, remember Paul's warning to take "captive every thought to make it obedient to Christ." (2 Corinthians 10:5 NIV) When enemy soldiers slip through your army's front lines, do you, as the commanding general, just let them go free, running amok and using up their rounds of ammo picking off your troops? Or do you stay vigilant and take them captive as soon as you can so they can't reduce your army's strength one man at a time? Lustful thoughts are dangerous. They can be life-threatening. If you give into them over and over again, you can end up in a place of despair, as my own precious sister's story shows. Please take these thoughts seriously and don't entertain them. Surrender them to God and actively start thinking about something wholesome. Find someone you can be accountable to. Satan likes to get you to feel isolated in your struggle against sin, because he knows that you are vulnerable to more sin if you think you're the only Christian girl out there fighting lustful thoughts.

THE HIDDEN DANGER OF ROMANCE NOVELS

The second big problem I dealt with as a single girl was, believe it or not, romance novels. Not harlequins – the sensual, secular paperbacks – but the romance novels by well-known Christian fiction writers that are sold in Christian bookstores. Whereas guys get their motors revved by something they see, girls' engines are usually fueled with emotional pictures that appeal to their desires for affection, security and protection from a man, the longing to be cherished. I found this out when I started reading Christian romances at the age of ten. Writers employ elements in a story that will keep the reader interested and reading all the way to the end. In romances, they use tantalizing scenes – a man flirting with a woman, touching her in intimate but not generally overtly sexual ways, bedroom scenes of married couples. Innuendo goes a long way. Writers can imply a lot without explicitly stating anything.

So when I was ten and a voracious reader looking for new books, I found myself entering a world of fascinating things that I didn't quite understand. But my curiosity was piqued and I kept reading. My parents were careful about what books they allowed in our home, and the romances I first read were bland and decent. But by the time I was thirteen, I was reading romance novels wherever I could pick them up – mostly in church libraries. And when I say read, I mean that I skimmed the novels, looking for the scenes mentioned above. I realized that I was getting a "high" from these skimmings; they gave me material (albeit skimpy) to fantasize about guys I was attracted to, to imagine scenarios where a guy showed me affection. I'd create the perfect romance novel setting in my mind: So-and-so would come sit down by me at a lakeshore or something, and we'd watch the moon rise, and he'd put his arm around me… I'd lean my head on his shoulder, and we'd talk for hours about how much he liked me and how beautiful he thought I was, and could I marry him someday – when I was a little older than thirteen?

I soon learned which Christian novelists wrote more racy stuff, and opted for their books over the tame, proper novels that had a good story but didn't contain much in the way of man-falls-in-love-with-woman-and-they-get-awfully-close-to-the-edge. The satisfaction I felt after reading these novels was really short-lived and mixed with guilt. Instinctively, I knew that I was wrongly feeding desires that were supposed to remain asleep until I met the man I would marry. Good desires, bad timing.

Obviously, I made my own choices, but I think my big diet of romance novels fed my appetite for crushes on guys (whom Jesse accurately described earlier as "losers") through my teen and young adult years. I had let my hunger for love and affection become aroused, and infatuations were a supposedly safe way to deal with my awakened heart. I was so wrong. I wasted so many hours both reading and thinking about stuff I wasn't ready for. This may sound shocking at first, but I think it has been rightly observed that romance novels, however religious in tone, are often just pornography for Christian women. They can generate lustful thoughts, which can lead to sinful actions.

Without realizing it at the time, I also developed a warped perspective of real life romance after reading and being wooed by the subtle message of romance novels: that the best romance happens before you get married (most novels end before the man and woman marry), that a great body is necessary to experience satisfying romance and unfailingly attract good looking men, and that it's okay to indulge in some of your desires with people you're not married to. The majority of novels don't deal with the reality of challenges within marriage, of raising children, of selfish spouses, short tempers, or tired wives who aren't interested in amour at the drop of a hat. In a ChristiaNet.com poll, "Many [of those polled] expressed concerns about these books causing damage to existing relationships by creating an 'unrealistic view of life and love.'" For some women, romance novels can set up expectations for a perfect husband and conflict-free relationship. When they discover that perfect men have never been in stock and that conflict is a natural part of life, they may become disillusioned and continue to discontentedly search for the sort of love that's only found between the pages of their novels.

Since becoming Mrs. Jost, I've found that real married life is unlike and far above what romance novels convey. I'm so glad! I'm grateful Jesse's imperfections are there to help rub off some of my many flaws and form me into a more godly woman. He's such an awesome guy, and so gracious with me. I'm thankful for opportunities to show selflessness and put his needs above my own… it's not always with a thankful spirit in the moment, but usually in hindsight. The love Jesse and I have for each other is better than any implied scene in a book, because ours is real. We have the wonderful privilege of making daily choices to love each other in a hundred different ways.

Until your romance becomes a reality for you – a man you have committed to for life – be cautious of the negative effects romance novels can have on your thought life and your beliefs. If romance novels encourage you to lust, to long even more intensely for something that is not yours yet, they are not worth your time reading.

I'm pulling for you! This is not an easy time of life. I know that. However long or short your season of singleness, may God give you the strength you need to keep guarding your heart and mind.

A WORD OF WARNING AND HOPE

Jesse: I want to end this chapter with a warning to both you guys and girls. When you put this book down, you're going to face the pressures and temptations that are the reality of life. You have an unseen enemy who hates you with a passion, doing everything he can to destroy you. This enemy is crafty and has had thousands of years of honing his craft. He knows how to make young people fall. He is willing to wait you out. He will not come at you with all his tricks at once, but will try to wear you down by getting you to make one little compromise after another. He can make dreadful poison look so appealing. Knowing how sexual purity and romantic relationships affect every other part of life, Satan would love to bring you down in these areas.

Physical intimacy and erotic love are some of God's greatest gifts to us. They are pictures of the kind of intimacy that God wants to have with us, infused with a taste of heaven. This gift has tremendous power for good. But anything that has power for good has equal power for evil. Sexuality gone rampant can sear and destroy unlike anything else. Think about the millions of broken homes, shattered hearts, devastated children, disintegrating bodies, not to mention the spiritual alienation from God. Satan wants to twist your God-given passions and desires for sex and romance, using your wrong choices to bring great destruction. The sad thing is, every temptation will seem harmless and inconsequential in the moment! Don't be deceived! Nobody who let their sex drive get out of control and create havoc deliberately thought they were choosing destruction. It always looks good and desirable in the moment – all part of Satan's plan.

I don't care if you write me off as out of touch with reality or an old-fashioned prude. But I do care deeply about every one of you who reads this book. I don't want you to have children who cry themselves to sleep because Mommy and Daddy hate each other. I don't want you to die a slow, cruel death from AIDS or a sexually transmitted disease. I don't want your future wives to feel like worthless trash because you are addicted to pornography. I don't want your future husbands to feel sick when they think about the physical intimacy you have shared with other men.

The enemy is going to tell you that immorality is no big deal – that a little touching, a little peek, a little fantasy isn't going to hurt anyone. That is his whole plan! Of course he's going to peddle his wares to you and tell you it's no big deal. Do you think anyone would bite if the enemy told the truth? "Uh, here, have a little peek at this pornography. It will give you a few minutes of pleasure, followed by days and months of guilt and alienation from God. It will warp your views on sex and women, and prevent you from ever being truly satisfied in life. Basically, the more you look at this stuff, the greater your hunger will be and the less pleasure you will have. But other than that, it's a great product!"

Right now you have a choice. You can surrender your love life to your Creator and receive from Him the strength you need to battle for what's right, and then in the end find blissful ecstasy, followed by total satisfaction. Or you can slowly give in to the enemy's temptations and fall into his trap. Every time you give in to lust, another link forms on a chain around you. You will become a slave, weeping bitterly as you watch yourself bring pain and heartache to those you love the most. Blessings and curses are before you. Choose life! Choose purity – choose God!

I'm not saying it will be easy. Not at all! Young men, you will have to fight valiantly to slay the dragon of lust. But your princess is so worth the fight! Young women, you are so precious to God! God made you with a tender vulnerability and feminine softness that makes a man willing to lay down his life to protect you. Your beauty and charms can inspire a guy unlike anything else in the world. But sadly, it is you women who too often get the brunt of the consequences lust brings. You have to fight for purity in your own way. Every time you dress provocatively or entice a man to do something immoral, you are contributing to a fire that may eventually consume you. Your heart, your mind, and your body belong to your future husband. Be diligent to protect them. Don't make yourself cheap or give away part of your treasure to a man who is not worthy of you.

Young people, purity will not happen by accident! It is a prize of great value, but it will come at a huge cost – withstanding the pressures of society, facing scorn for not buying into Satan's game plan, or ridicule for not fitting in with the crowd. You'll need a will of iron determination to make it to your wedding day pure and whole. Purity comes at high cost. But the cost cannot begin to compare to the price you will pay if you stop fighting. Your only alternative to fighting for purity and true romance is to give in and let your life follow the natural course of disaster that is devouring millions of other young people your age.

Don't lose hope. No matter what you have done in the past, there is always hope for the future. God can cleanse your heart and mind and give you a fresh start. Don't fall for Satan's lie that tells you, "You've already given in before, you might as well this time, too." Each time you give in will only make life worse. Another small compromise might not seem like a big deal, but it is a step in the wrong direction, and the more steps you take, the further you will be from the delight and satisfaction that God wants to give you.

Don't give up! It's not worth the pain. Make Christ the Lord of your life, and He will reward you beyond what you could ever dream of. Someday you will be able to lay down your sword and take off your armor and enjoy the sweet comfort and delight of true intimacy. You will discover with a shock of delight that the greatest pleasure is found in purity and holiness. As you learn to be intimate with the love of your life, you'll earnestly desire to be purged of your impurities and infidelities – to be cleansed by the refining fire of the Holy Spirit. The less you have to hide the more you will long to be known.

Experienced God's way, sex leads to a selfless giving to one another, and to the joy of becoming one with your spouse. However, if you abuse this gift, giving in to every selfish impulse, you will become enslaved within the prison of yourself, unable to enjoy God's gift when the time comes. You will be like the man in the story that began this chapter, who, instead of dying, becomes a lifeless wraith. His existence is marked by craving but never real satisfaction. When he does enter a beautiful garden where he can touch and eat anything he wants, the flowers wilt from his touch. But it doesn't matter – there is no more beauty for a person enslaved by lust, only insatiable craving.

CHAPTER 11

BE SATISFIED BY GOD

In the poignant book, *A Severe Mercy*, Sheldon Vanauken recounts the story of his love for his wife, Jean, or Davey, as he tenderly called her. These two reached as close a relationship as is possible for pagans to achieve. They loved each other deeply, sharing a rare depth of intimacy. God drew them to Himself and they both became followers of the Master. However, Davey's spiritual growth progressed much faster than Sheldon's. He grew to resent how deeply she loved God and the amount of time and energy she was pouring into His service. Sheldon became bitter… until his precious wife contracted a fatal disease. She passed away quickly.

Sheldon was devastated. He turned to his friend, C. S. Lewis, for counsel and comfort. Lewis gently reminded Sheldon how critically important it is for God to have first place, and how this tragedy might have been a severe form of God's mercy.

True love is selfless. To be selfless, we must be satisfied by God.

He alone can meet our deepest emotional needs. We seek and desire, but when we acquire earthly goods or human relationships, they will inevitably fail to satisfy us at some point. We'll turn and criticize the thing we thought we wanted – the thing we thought would satisfy.

God knows how critical it is for our well-being that He is the center our lives revolve around. Knowing this, He will allow us to go through trials in order to bring us back to the place where He reigns supreme in our hearts.

My heart is deceitful, always finding more love for things or people than for God. I really love Heidi and earnestly desire to love her as Christ loved the church. Yet if I don't first look to God to meet my needs, my love for Heidi can turn into a hurtful, ugly thing. Fears, insecurities, and jealousies creep in and wreak havoc. It's unfair to shoulder anyone with the terrible burden of meeting your deepest needs. No person, no matter how godly, beautiful, or fun they are, can meet that need! If you look to a specific person to fulfill you, you will always eventually come away hurt, critical, and disappointed. Your love may grow cold and you'll give up on that person, looking wistfully for someone else to satisfy. Or you'll grit your teeth and keep a lifeless and miserable marriage together.

If you desire marriage (I'm assuming you do, if you've read this far), prepare for it first by diligently seeking after God. The closer you are to God – the more you love Him – the closer you will be to your spouse and the more vibrant your love will be for each other. I can't say it strongly enough: Do all that you can to keep God at the center. Make sure that He is the foundation of your love and commitment. Nothing else will stand the test of time. Beauty fades, personalities change, money disappears, and human security can vanish in a moment. But a marriage that has God at its center will last and be a thing of beauty for the world to see.

So when you find yourself madly in love with someone, but you aren't ready for marriage, view this as the perfect opportunity to prepare for marriage. Learn to die to this desire, to completely surrender that special guy or girl to God, and make Christ first in your life. There are many times in marriage where you must be wholly selfless in your giving of love. Perhaps your spouse will be sick or facing an emotional struggle and you will have to love without expecting anything in return. Until you know how to be satisfied by Christ alone, you're not ready to love a spouse the way God wants you to.

At this point you may be thinking, "That sounds nice, but how can I be satisfied by God?" How can we be satisfied by an invisible, non-physical being, when our needs are so physical? It won't make sense until you try it. It's like a new food – your friend can try to explain how the flavors will hit the taste buds and how the brain will interpret it as pleasure, but the best way to experience the food is to just taste it! That is what I suggest to you – taste and see that God is good.

I don't understand how God wired us anymore than I understand the mechanics of taste, but I do know that those who look to God are satisfied by Him in a way that nothing else will satisfy. Just as God made the tongue to experience pleasure in a variety of textures and flavors (and the tongue is happiest when it's tasting good food), so He also made our souls to be able to experience the pleasures of communion with Him. We were created to enjoy God. Our soul has pleasure receptors that are only satisfied by Him (Psalm 16:11).

So how can we taste God? What can we do to feel His presence? In my own experience, I've found five primary ways: prayer, gratitude, worship, Bible reading, and nature.

PRAYER
Jesus told us plainly that whoever asks shall be given and whoever seeks shall find (Matthew 7:7). He was talking about a relationship with God. Prayer is the first step in tasting God. Prayer is how we acknowledge our need for God; it's our reminder that if we want to enter God's pres-

ence we must do it on His terms. If you want God, simply ask! Pursue Him wholeheartedly! God's presence is always there, but prayer opens our spiritual ears and the mouth of our soul.

Prayer is also a time of training our minds to see life from God's perspective. It is so easy to let our stress and anxieties cloud our vision and lose sight of the things that really matter. Time spent before God's throne breaks the spell of our delusions and clarifies our vision. We see how beautiful God really is, how worthy He is to be trusted, and how satisfying a relationship with Him can be.

Guys, grab this time to prepare for the day when you will be the spiritual leader of your own home. Grow intimate with God now. Learn to be a man on your knees, a man who seeks to rely completely on God. Nothing brings security to a wife like seeing that her husband knows how to cast himself in total reliance on God and is willing to sacrifice whatever is necessary in order to do God's will. Become the type of man God wants you to be. Don't wait for a wife to influence you toward godliness.

GRATITUDE

We have a terrible propensity for self-deception, because our perception of life is so limited and easily warped. We can begin to form a godless view of our world, and it starts when we take our gifts for granted – as if they are our natural right. In this state God seems so far removed and we think that because we have closed our eyes and can't see God, He must not be there. But the closing of our eyes to what God has done does not remove Him at all. It does, however, remove the joy and satisfaction that He wants to fill us with.

C. S. Lewis said that "Pride…is the great anti-God state of mind", because pride is always looking at those who are beneath it. But God is so far above us that to see Him, we must look up! We must recognize the fact that our every breath is a gift from God, that He alone keeps our hearts beating. We humans have no intrinsic life source in us; everything comes to us as a gift. The antidote to pride is realizing our true state and being thankful for all we've been given. Simply counting God's gifts to us shows us how dependent we are on Him, but it also reveals how good God is. With the reminder of our dependency comes a renewed confidence in God's ability to provide.

Gratitude is the opener of our spiritual eyes. When we see the goodness around us as gifts rather than a natural right, our eyes are drawn to the Giver. It has been my experience that the presence of God seems most real when I am giving thanks. I think this is why Paul tells us to "In everything give thanks" (I Thessalonians 5:18). If you are feeling empty, look around! God's gifts are everywhere to be seen - in the sunsets, in the cool summer breeze, in sensations of touch and sound, in the arms of a loved one. God is good. It is not His fault that we don't always notice.

WORSHIP

We were made to worship; this is reflected in the fact that we are constantly on the lookout for someone or something to adore and place our affections in. But eventually we get bored. No matter how great the person or thing was at first, it becomes commonplace. People disappoint us and thrills wear off. So the search continues. But those who discover God have a continual feast. He's the only object of worship that will always satisfy and not disappoint! We worship God when our eyes are open to His beauty and majesty and we are in awe of who He is and what He has done. It's the deepest, richest, most fulfilling experience known to man.

We can worship in silent awe, when the Holy Spirit fills us with His presence and opens the eyes of our souls. Or worship can be found in song. The psalmist says that God "inhabits the praises of his people" (Psalm 22:3). Music seems to have a spiritual quality to it, an incredible power to move us emotionally. Music takes the truth of the mind and makes it real for the emotions. We can know that God is near and that He is loving, but singing about these truths transforms them into whole-person experiences and fills our hearts with joy. There are so many powerful worship songs and hymns that have comforted Christians and given them spiritual power. If you are feeling empty, find a good worship CD or a hymn book and start singing. Let the words speak truth to your emotions, and begin to behold the awesome beauty and holiness of your God!

BIBLE READING

God's Word is not just information to be studied; it is actual spiritual food. When you sit down to a meal, you may know every ingredient that is in the food and you may know where it came from, but you won't experience the pleasure of the food or receive its nourishment until you eat it. If you stop eating because you think you know all about the food, you will starve. So it is with God's Word. We read not merely for mental knowledge, (although that aspect is important) but especially for spiritual sustenance.

But it's not enough to simply read the Bible. Like food, it also has to be digested. When we eat, our bodies convert food into strength and material to repair our systems. In a similar way, we need to digest the food and break it down for our spiritual body to be repaired. We digest God's Word by meditating on it.

As we ponder God's Word and try to understand what it means, our minds are changed and His light is shed on us, so we begin to see ourselves and our situations more accurately. Once we understand, we need to seek to have our wills and emotions conformed to God's truth. I know from experience the power the memorized Word has to fill my soul with joy and usher me into God's presence. Sadly, I also know from experience the emptiness and doubt that can cloud my soul when I do not feed regularly. As you read and meditate on God's Word, don't forget why you're doing it. Don't let it become an empty spiritual ritual you do to feel better about yourself. When you pick up a Bible, invite the Holy Spirit to be your guide, and ask Him to use the words on the page to reveal the living God.

NATURE

God has not only revealed His nature in the pages of a book, He has also revealed Himself in Nature. When you experience the natural world, you get a taste of God. The majesty of canyons and mountains is a reflection of God's majesty and holiness. The awesome power in lightning and thunderstorms is a little taste of God's power. The autumn wind and the summer breeze reflect His Holy Spirit. The variety of animals and landscapes reveal God's creativity. The ever changing beauty of the sunsets is a sample of His extravagance. When you surround yourself with God's creation, it gives the soul a wide open place to breathe and stretch. Being absorbed with our needs, anxieties, and problems is very stuffy and suffocating. But standing on the edge of a valley or before a mountain ridge seems to put life into perspective. Both Heidi and I love to stand on top of a hill and let the magnitude of creation make us feel small. G. K. Chesterton noted that for Alice to enter Wonderland, she must make herself small. Nature has a way of humbling us, and places our focus on the wonder of God. God is able to fill your lonely heart. Come to Him with your mouth wide open and He will fill it!

GRACE IN THE MIDST OF MORNING SICKNESS

During our first month of marriage, Heidi had PMS. I figured once was enough. I cheerfully said, "I'll fix that!" My solution worked. Unfortunately, the side effects included extreme nausea – morning sickness that couldn't read time and caused frequent re-runs of her food… if you know what I mean. When we found out she was pregnant, we were thrilled. But shortly after that, much of our exuberance went down the toilet along with scrambled contents of Heidi's stomach. While Heidi vomited around the clock, I wondered what happened to my perky, affectionate wife. One day I take her in my arms and she melts into my embrace and I feel like the most romantic guy around. The next day I take her in my arms to kiss her and she has to run to the bathroom to throw up and I feel about as romantic as a moldy piece of chicken.

Most of Heidi's attention was zeroed in on keeping food down and I felt left out. During this time I was learning what true love really is. God again showed me that He is able to satisfy. We weathered the storm and I was able to win even more of Heidi's heart by my feeble attempt at selfless love. By the way, our John-Michael has been worth every minute of the nausea. (**Heidi:** He sure has, and so has Sophia! And Jesse was my hero – he made meals whenever he could, brought me breakfast in bed, and just held my hand and prayed for me when he would much rather have held all of me.)

A huge step you can take toward fulfilling romance is learning to be emotionally fulfilled by God right now, right where He has you. If you can't find contentment now, marriage will not provide a lasting solution.

I have been waiting for my future spouse for years, but it's a lonely and often difficult wait. Sometimes I really doubt whether there are any truly godly potential mates out there. Is this long, patient "battle" worth it?

I really feel for you single people who have waited into your late 20s or 30s or 40s. I can only imagine how lonely it must get. But what I do know is that God is not only the God of the married, he is also the God of the single. When God takes away or withholds a gift or an ability that most people have, such as marriage, or the ability to walk, it leaves a hole – a void. But if you are willing, God is able to take that empty spot and fill it with his joy. He is the only one who can bring true, deep lasting joy. Anytime we feel like we have to have some earthly item or we can't be happy, it is an insult to God because He is always there and ready to fill you.

I don't know why God has withheld marriage from you, but I do know the nature and character of God and that He only has your best in mind (Jeremiah 29:11). I don't say this glibly or feel like I have a right to preach to you from this side of a honeymoon. But any person who feels like they are missing something that they rightfully deserve has two choices. They can shake their fists at God and miserably chafe against their circumstances until they get their way, or they can submit to God's will for their life and look to Him to be satisfied.

You may be single, but in one respect you are no different from someone who is married. You both have the same choice to either look at what you don't have and wish you had it. Or you can look at what you do have and be thankful.

Is the waiting worthwhile? To answer this, I guess you'd also have to ask: Is the alternative to waiting – compromising yourself sexually or romantically – worthwhile? Erotic love has the same power to damage or bring bliss as it did when you were younger. Every person who has compromised and violated God's design by willful rebellion has regretted it deeply. You can jump off a cliff hoping that this time gravity will change, but your odds are not good. The consequences of going against God's natural laws are inevitable. Not all marriage experiences are wonderful. As I'm sure you've seen many times, a bad marriage can be a miserable thing. God really does know what is best. Wait for romantic involvement, but don't feel like you have to wait for life!

God always has a purpose in the things He will give you to do. No matter what state of life you're in, you have the choice to look to God and be satisfied or look elsewhere and be disappointed.

Heidi: Our hearts sure go out to you. We have the utmost respect for men and women who purpose to stay pure and wait for God to reveal their future mate. Jesse and I married when we were 23 and 22. We didn't have long years to wait, as some of our friends have had. Sometimes I wonder, "Why us, and why not them?" but only God has the answer to that. And that is where your greatest encouragement can be found: the knowledge that God knows best. Your surrender to His guidance is really admirable. We have so much respect for people who are willing to wait – even if it means many years – and seek to "do love" God's way.

It is hard to say anything without it coming across as flippant words from two married people. But please know that we hope you will stay strong and continue to wait. Your example of trust in God for a spouse is an inspiration and strength to far more people than you realize. During my short wait for Jesse, I was really encouraged by several single friends who were still waiting for a mate, while at the same time pouring themselves into active ministry and work.

When you first decided to wait for God to bring your future spouse, you believed He had a better plan and knew better than you did what you needed. Does He still? That is a question you will have to answer between Him and you.

Jesse: One last thing - don't believe people who tell you that you are still single because God doesn't think you are ready for marriage. When God brings marriage to you, He will give you what you need. Singleness is not a punishment or correctional institution for those who aren't mature enough for marriage. I know that singleness has its own blessings and benefits, but there are people who have actually earned the "fulfilled single" badge and are much more worthy to write on the subject.

CHAPTER 12

DISCOVER YOUR CALLING

A woman was unloading her golf clubs when she met a fellow golfer. "How did you do?" she asked the man.

"Not that great," he answered, "I shot a 70."

"Really?" she exclaimed, "That's pretty good!"

The man smiled, "Maybe, but I hope to beat that score on my second hole."

I used to think that joke was funny... until I went golfing. My brother Jonathan suggested we go golfing after work one day. I thought it sounded like fun. We had gone golfing earlier in the year – my first time on the links in fifteen years – and I shot a 62. Pretty good, eh? I should maybe tell you that it was only a nine-hole course. I was eager to improve my score. Well, this particular day I got to feel golf's awesome power to humiliate and strip a person of their sense of masculinity, self-worth, and... pretty much all dignity.

On my first hole I shot an 11 on a par three. I decided that was a good practice hole. I ran back to the beginning and started all over. I should have just kept running back to Jon's van, satisfied to revel in the fact that I once shot a 62. On my mulligan of the first hole, Jon stopped my ball that was going to skip way past the green and I, thanks to the "human hazard", got a double bogey.

I'd say the weak parts of my game are my putting, chip shots, fairway shots, and drives. My strength in golf is my ability to press the tee into the ground. However, where I really struggled was with my drives... most of my putts went further. The rare time I did get some distance, my ball was directionally challenged. It was especially embarrassing on hole four when we decided to play past a group of four seniors who appeared to have taken up the sport recently. Jon stepped up to the tee and belted a mammoth drive that hooked right towards the green. The group of seniors was impressed. I strode confidently to the tee, took a few practice swings, and whacked the ball. It soared a majestic twelve yards with a sharp hook into the pond on the left.

The Four were kind. They said, "Relax! You seem nervous." (I wasn't nervous. I was just lousy.) Jon gave me another ball. I asked the Four to close their eyes. I tried to keep my swing free and easy and then swung hard, determined to get out of there. Splash! The ball followed the same course as the last ball. I'm sure at this point the Four were regretting their decision to let us play through. They told me again to relax and that there was no rush. (Now I was nervous.) Jon gave me a third ball. I teed off for the third time and this time it stayed straight. I grabbed a two iron, thanked them and got out of there as fast as possible.

I need to tell you about my golf swing: it's kind of a cross between an Aztec warrior machete slash and a baseball swing, and it brings up more dirt than a politician.

It was a long afternoon. I tried everything. I'd swing hard and the ball would go bouncing about twenty feet…oftentimes less. And what made it worse was that when I got close to the hole, I would try for an easy swing and then I would suddenly get distance! On the last hole it all came together. I'm not talking about my game, though. I'm talking about the pile of mud, grass, broken tee, and my ball that made it "the whole nine yards" to the women's tee-off marker. On the course, I broke two golf clubs (the only driver that we'd brought and Jon's two-iron). So I'm not as enthusiastic about golf as I was the first time. At least I know that I really left my mark on the game!

Golf is not my calling. Thankfully, when God calls you to do something, He will call you in an area where you are gifted and have a passion for it. As a single, you don't have to feel like your life is on hold until you are married. God always has a work for you to do, a life calling that He wants you to fulfill. Pour all your energy into serving God and advancing His kingdom. You'll always find the most fulfillment in doing what God made you to do and in becoming the person you were created to be.

I don't think I am suggesting anything new by saying that doing God's will is a good way to spend your life. But while most of you already know that, what is not so clear is knowing exactly what God's will is for your life. This subject raises a ton of questions and can cause a lot of anxiety in searching young people. Sometimes we fear we'll miss God's will for us – that we will seek and not find. How can we know that we are in the center of God's will? How can we discern God's will? Is it through signs or soggy wool sweaters? Is God's will found in carefully thinking through the options, or by shutting off the mind and following your heart? I have no desire to stand here in the place of a prophet and declare God's will to you. But as a fellow Christian who's spent his life so far trying to do the will of God, I'd like to share with you some of the principles that I've found helpful. I will also share some of the highlights of how God has led me and my thought process behind my decisions.

GOD IS MY CREATOR

Meditating on this truth has probably helped soothe my fears in this area more than anything else. It is amazing to ponder that God planned me and carefully crafted me together. I've spent a lot of time over the years crafting things from decks and additional rooms to delicate things like origami and intricate scroll work. I love creating things and I have a certain fondness for my creations. When I think that God invested His time, energy, and love to create me, I'm filled with wonder. I also realize that the creator of an object decides the purpose for it. I have confidence that I am here for a reason, that God has a purpose and design for my life. He created me to accomplish specific things in His work of transforming and redeeming His world.

GOD HAS A REVEALED WILL

There are many basic principles revealed in God's Word that God has given to help us determine His will. God wants us to rejoice always, pray always, and always be thankful (1 Thessalonians 5:16-18); we can be confident that complaining is never God's will. God wants us to serve people in need, including widows and orphans (James 1:27). He tells me to make sure I am diligent to provide spiritual and physical nourishment for those under me (1 Timothy 5:8). If, then, a job or opportunity prevents me from fulfilling these obligations to meet the needs of my wife and children, I can feel free to turn it down without a fear of missing God's will. We know that God's will is for us to spend time in God's Word, memorizing it and meditating on it (Joshua 1:8), and to abstain from things that cause us to compromise (1 Peter 2:12). God clearly wants us to spend time in prayer and have a general dependence on Him (Matthew 6).

I spend a lot of time writing, studying, and preparing for talks, but I know that I have a responsibility to provide income for the needs of my family. God has never failed to provide for us. When our resources are low, God provides work, often through my younger brother Jonathan, who owns a handyman business. It is a great fit, because he believes in what I do and is very understanding of my need for time to write and travel. I try to make the most of my time at home, but also stay open to work opportunities. When God provides work, I take it, knowing with confidence that I am where God wants me. When He provides opportunities to speak, I feel completely justified in taking the time I need to prepare. God is our ultimate provider and where He leads He also supplies. When I seek his kingdom first, in other words, make God's priorities my own, God promises to take care of all our needs. (Matthew 6:33)

God directs through our gifts and desires

Just as a craftsman will design a tool with the specific characteristics necessary to fulfill its function, so God has gifted you for the purpose you were created to live out.

In my early teen years, I loved spending hours in the workshop creating pieces of art with my scroll saw. When I was fourteen, my Dad stepped down from being a pastor and went off salary so that he could devote more time to disciple and equip his family. God used my love of woodwork to help provide for our family. A woman discovered my work at a farmer's market and asked our family to make 110 bed headboards for a new lodge that was going up in Waterton Lakes National Park. My mom designed the inserts for the headboards – each room in the lodge needed a different design – and I cut them out on my scroll saw.

When I graduated from twelve grades of home school, God continued to guide me through my desires and interests. I spent the next few years at home studying my passions of literature, church history, philosophy, and Christian apologetics. I chose to study at home for a few reasons. It was much cheaper for one thing. I knew that academic degrees in my areas of interest are not really helpful in earning money, so I did not feel justified in spending a lot of money to get them. It was the information I wanted, not the degree, and I was able to get that information much more affordably at home. (I didn't have to pay for room and board, or for a professor's salary. Some careers do require college degrees and if my gifts and desires were in one of these areas I would have been open to a university or college.) I had the motivation and drive to study at home; I didn't need to be driven by deadlines. I was able to study these subjects from different perspectives rather than only get the "authorized" perspective of the Bible school or college. I bought books (often used copies) by a variety of different professors and scholars, and then weighed the pros and cons of each view as I read them. For me, I felt this was a much more balanced way to learn.

I also believed that God wanted me home to be able to serve my family. Life is so much more than academics, and I learned a lot about real life by spending those extra years at home helping with chores and renovation projects and the home schooling of the younger ones. I never felt like my family was holding me back. I loved having these opportunities to serve. During this time, I earned money by doing various jobs for farmers and also working at a seed cleaning plant. Whenever I needed work, God provided.

Feel free to pursue the things that you love. On the movie, "Chariots of Fire," Eric Liddell tells his sister, "God also made me fast, and when

I run, I feel His pleasure." God used Eric's love for running to place him in a position of tremendous influence. So many people feel that if they surrender their life to God, He will ask them to give up what they most enjoy doing. What they fail to realize is that they take pleasure in the things they do because God gifted them to do those things. When a person loves making music or has a passion for a science, they are simply responding to the way God made them. When you surrender your desires to God, this frees you to enjoy your passions without becoming a slave to them.

You will only find the pursuit of your goals fulfilling if you have first made the choice to live for God's glory and use your gifts for Him. When your goals and dreams are pursued for selfish glory or fame, the attainment will be profoundly empty. History is full of examples of people who pursued their dreams as ends in themselves and found they didn't satisfy. But those who pursue their dreams out of a desire to serve God and honor Him find life very satisfying, whether they achieved all they set out to do or not.

GOD IS SOVEREIGN

When I recognize that I have been created by God, I also realize how much of my life has already been predetermined by God. There are many aspects of me that I had no choice in: my parents and ancestors, the size of my family, my time in history, or the country where I was born. When I see all the circumstances that God has had control over, it is easier to trust Him to continue to lead through circumstances. I've found that God does provide direction if I follow the advice of Proverbs 3:5-6, "Trust in the Lord with all your heart and lean not on your own understanding; in all your ways acknowledge Him, and He shall direct your path." But He doesn't simply give me vague, easy-to-miss signs or direct me to strange Bible verses that I have to take out of context. God is so much more powerful than that!

I remember several months after I was turned down by the first father, I had a chance to see his daughter at an event. I was still interested in her, and the night before I saw her I was tormented by thoughts of her. I prayed so much that night, trying to give the whole situation to God and also seeking to discern if she still might play a role in my future. I prayed, "God, if she is still the girl I'm going to marry, help her to be really friendly to me when I see her. But if she's not, help her to be cold toward me." Some prayer! The next day when I made eye contact with her, she quickly looked away and didn't return my smile. My heart sank. Later I had a chance to talk to her and this time she was friendly. I didn't know which response was the divine sign.

Thankfully, God is so much more sovereign than we give Him credit for and when we trust Him to direct us, He does more than just leave faint impressions and enigmatic clues. God is not trying to make things difficult or cryptic. Oftentimes the problem is not that we don't know what God wants, but that we do and we're trying to avoid it. Your job is to say yes to the right opportunities and be discerning in turning down the ones that cause you to compromise.

I believe seeking God's will means that we exercise discernment by using our minds in making a wise choice. Our job is to have an attitude of surrender to His will for us and to make sure we have carefully and prayerfully thought through the issues involved, and then trust Him to lead through His all-knowing providence. When my desire is to do His will, He makes His will abundantly clear through my circumstances. He has the power to open and close doors. Our job is simply to stay alert and open to these opportunities and then trust God's sovereign orchestrating of events.

In my search for the life mate that God had for me, I was turned down by two fathers. The only reason both of them gave for saying no was that they simply didn't have peace. When I finally was given the green light with Heidi, I knew without a doubt that this was God's will, because if it wasn't, God would have shut the door again.

I'm not saying that whatever God allows us to do is His will. We can be disobedient, foolish, and willful, and God will let us suffer the consequences. What I'm saying is that when we allow God to lead and truly look to Him for guidance, and carefully weigh our options in light of His Word, He will direct our steps through His sovereign control of circumstances.

Pursue excellence wherever your interests lie. Your responsibility is to become skilled in what you do and diligent in your relationship with Him, and God will provide the opportunities to use your gifts. Ask God to expand your ministry and He will. Like my dad often says, we take care of the depth and God will take care of the breadth. God is looking for people who are available so He can show Himself strong through them. You'll be amazed to see how God can use your gifts for His purposes.

God has opened so many doors to use the gifts He has given me. Those years of study at home have reaped huge dividends. I've spoken at camps and to different youth groups across Canada, and have taught apologetics at a college level. I've even debated the resurrection with an atheist on national television. It isn't easy. I often feel so nervous that I come close to throwing up, but I cry out to God each time before I speak. "God, you gave me this opportunity – you created me for this purpose. Please give me your strength and your words. I've been diligent to do as much preparation as I can. Now I look to you to fill me with your Spirit. Give me your words so that they can be used to accomplish your work."

Life is so fulfilling when you are in the center of God's will. He knows your future and controls the events of your life. He is looking for a willing heart. If you desire to do His will, He will make things clear. When you have to make decisions, don't simply look for signs. God wants you to use your mind to make a wise choice. Become familiar with His Word, so that you are familiar with what is on His heart. If you have a passion for something that is in line with God's revealed will, commit it to Him and begin pursuing it. He'll direct you through your circumstances.

TAKE THE NEXT STEP

When you are not sure of all the details and feel like the future looks foggy, take inspiration from Sir William Osler. Osler, who lived in the late 19th century, was one of the most famous physicians of his time, but as a young man he was drowning in his studies and on the verge of a nervous breakdown. Then he read some advice from Thomas Carlyle that changed his life: "Our main business is not to see what lies dimly at a distance, but to do what clearly lies at hand." Osler went on to be knighted by the king of England; he also organized the John Hopkins School of Medicine and became Regius professor of Medicine at Oxford. God will always give you light for the next step. But make sure you take it! You don't have to wait until all the details are in place or have a complete vision all mapped out. But you do need to do the next thing.

When God gives you a task, it will be very clear at the outset, but sometimes as difficulties set in, you may begin to doubt. Don't give up! Don't doubt in the night what God has made clear in the day. God only has your best in mind. Give Him your life, make yourself available to Him, and He will take care of the rest.

Don't let your talents go to waste. Someday we will all stand before our Creator and give an account of what we did with what we were given. And to whom much is given, much will be required. But there is also great reward waiting for those who give their gifts and abilities to God and spend their life in the service of their Master.

Chapter 13

TRUST GOD TO KNOW WHAT'S BEST

Trust is so important to God – it is vital for a relationship with Him. But trust is easy to talk about, and often hard to do. When Heidi and I had been married for only eight months, I had my faith tested.

Things were going wonderfully. I had a good job, a comfortable amount in the bank account, a beautiful wife who was seven and a half months pregnant, a library full of delicious books to devour, and a wish/needs list the length of my thumbnail. Did I trust God? Absolutely! I mean, I could lose my job, break an arm, buy a hundred books, and still have enough to live on for months. In this position, I was what you'd call a man of great faith. I had unshakable confidence in God to provide.

Right.

This all changed one November day. Life had settled into a very comfortable pace. Work drywalling with my brother was going great. Heidi and I were getting more excited about the arrival of our little one with each new blanket and bootie we received. Life was normal, in an exciting sort of way...until one wrong turn sent my wife and me into a month of turmoil. We had just come out of a bookstore in the city and got into our blue Dodge Spirit. I pulled out into an intersection to make a left turn, and waited till I thought the coast was clear. The only problem was that a pickup truck in the oncoming lane was also making a left turn and obstructed my view. I pulled out only to see a fast approaching minivan. I slammed on my brakes, and then Heidi and I watched helplessly as the van crashed into the front of our car. We heard that sickening sound of metal crunching. The impact knocked the passenger wheel off its tie-rod, so the car flopped like a fish while I maneuvered it to the nearest curb. Standing by the car, I shivered from more than the cold while we waited for the police to arrive. They were very helpful...told me how to pay my ticket and how this would affect my driving record. The ticket was the hard part. At the time, it seemed like the accident was unavoidable – I simply couldn't see the van, but the ticket dumped the burden of blame on my shoulders. I felt so stupid for putting Heidi and our unborn baby in harm's way.

Suddenly this Man of Great Faith felt like a "lost boy of great nerves." All the cars I saw later that day had oil dripping from their fangs and daggers for pinstripes. Our car was totaled. Because the accident was my fault, insurance didn't cover our vehicle's damages. Suddenly finances became a huge deal. We needed to buy a new vehicle and work out a settlement with the other driver.

Before the collision I had "unshakable" confidence in God to provide for our needs, but the oft-repeated soundtrack of crunching metal blocked out that "Still Small Voice" speaking confidence to me. I felt scared and alone, unprepared for meeting the needs of my wife and a newborn, and for the job of finding another vehicle. It seemed as if the dark realities – or, I should say, possibilities – of life had ripped away my protection and thrown me out into the harsh winds of an uncertain future. I was experiencing firsthand the Houdini act that riches can pull on people. Anxious and afraid were now the top two on my list of emotional ingredients.

During this time, I was asked to teach in our church on the great commission (Matthew 28). I decided to focus on the "teaching [new disciples] to obey everything I have commanded" portion of the text. What were all these things God had commanded? In searching through Matthew, one command stood out and was repeated most often: "Do not worry... Do not be afraid." Wow. How did I miss that? When the God of the universe stepped into our world, the message that He spoke most clearly and frequently was that we must trust Him.

All through Scripture, God is making it clear we have to trust Him. Men who trust Him are praised and held up as examples; those who doubt are sternly rebuked. The Bible is serious about this issue. Faith and belief are repeatedly stressed as critical to our walk with God and trust is the key element in both of these. In His Word, God's message could not be clearer: "Trust Me and live like it!"

Why do we not get this? In our self-examinations, how often do fear and worry grab our attention as sins that need to be repented of? Not often. Instead, they're our pet sins, expected and accepted without a second thought. Why is this? It seems to me that because this issue of trust is so important to God and dear to His heart, our enemy works overtime to keep us blinded to it. Satan's first lie – that God was not trustworthy – was an assault on this truth.

But does God, like us, wink at fear and worry? When Jesus' disciples were in the midst of a violent storm out at sea, they were scared. It was understandable, right? Growing up in a fishing community, they knew the danger of the Sea of Galilee; they had probably all lost family members to it at one time or another. The sea was their symbol for terror. But when He saw them, Jesus didn't say "I understand. Your feelings are to be expected." No, He sternly rebuked them. God doesn't justify or overlook anxiety and fear; they are insults to His character and often symptoms of deeper problems.

When God calls us to trust, He is not patting us reassuringly on the back, "Don't worry – nothing bad will happen. Everything will go just like you want it to." No, He is demanding that in the midst of our disappointments we trust Him to know what is best, acknowledging that He is sovereign enough to execute His will. If you have a genie concept of God (i.e. if you rub Him with the right prayer, you'll get what you want), then you won't find release from your anxieties. But when you realize that God is the supreme King who bends His knee to no one, and that He loves you enough to use difficult things to accomplish good in your life, then you'll find a release from earthly fears and gain the courage you need to face life's trials.

I haven't learned my lessons well. I have worried about many things these last few years, and have found myself scratching my head and asking God why. Each time God repeats the command that He gives to each of us, "Trust Me!"

One night not long after our car accident, I was on my way home from work, feeling the weight of financial pressures and sensing that everything was going wrong. That morning I had just found out that the van we recently bought had an engine with a cracked head and it could take thousands of dollars fix the problem. It seemed like God was at odds with me. Then a song on the radio caught my attention. It was about the little footprints of a son following behind his father and how they changed the father's perspective on life. The melody calmed my frayed emotions and I began to think about John-Michael, who was nestled in the safety of Heidi's womb. As I thought about this little life, every other earthly possession faded into the background. I got a taste of father love. My child truly meant more to me than anything in the world. While I was realizing this, God reminded me, "This father love that you feel for a little baby is only a tiny taste of my love for you. You know how you would do anything to help your little one. Just think how much more I, the sovereign Lord, of the universe am willing and able to help you!" The thought was a warm blanket against a harsh wind. I broke down and cried.

In the end, God provided through the generosity of my in-laws. They took the engine apart and repaired the engine for a fraction of the cost I was expecting.

God is worthy of our trust. He has promised to never leave us nor forsake us. He will always be there giving you strength and carefully monitoring every trial that comes your way. You will not be given more than you are able to bear.

Don't let worry and fear be the overlooked vices that come between you and God. In whatever you are going through, listen to and obey the stern and gentle words of your all-powerful Creator, "Do not worry! Do not be afraid! Be strong and courageous! Trust Me. I know better than you, and I will always be with you. I will provide all that you need: I am the Lord your God!"

In my most difficult struggles to be satisfied and content as a single person, my greatest help was meditating on who God is. I saw that He is my all-powerful Creator, that He is Lord of the universe and that no purpose of His can be thwarted.

HE IS INFINITE IN LOVE

He wants what is best for you. He wants to satisfy you with good things. He loves you like a good Father. I want to do anything I can to protect little Johnny-Mike and Sophia, and provide for their every need. Then to realize that my love for them is just a tiny taste of God's love for us – that thought is truly overwhelming!

HE IS INFINITE IN WISDOM

Not only does our God want what is best, but He knows better than anyone else what that "best" is. He knows what you want in a spouse even better than you do and He knows what you need in a spouse. He created you with all of your unique attributes and He created a person to complement you in every way. He also knows when both of you are truly ready to come together. You have such a limited perspective: You can't see behind the scenes to discern what an attractive certain someone is really like, or the person they will change into, or the trials and struggles yet to come for both of you. But God does, and He knows who is best suited to face life with you.

The night before I approached the first girl's father, I lost a lot of sleep because I was overwhelmed with questions about all the issues I just mentioned. I realized how little I really knew this girl and lifelong commitment to her was suddenly a scary thought. Then when the answer came back as a "no", I was so blessed by the song, "You Know Better Than I" from the movie *Joseph: King of Dreams*. I rested in the fact that my God really did know better than I did and that He would work all things for good.

And boy, did He ever!

HE IS INFINITE IN POWER

God is in complete control of every detail of the universe; there is not even an atom outside His sovereign rule. Therefore, God not only wants what is best and knows what truly is best, He also has the power to bring it to pass! If He has the power to create you and to fling this universe into existence out of nothing, then He has the power to put you with a spouse who will be all you can want and more. But He will not force you to do His will. You can't live this life any way you want and expect Him to bless it. If you want God to bless you with a godly precious husband or wife, then you must strive to become the type of person that God will find worthy of entrusting with such a gem.

If you surrender your desires to God and wait for His timing, He has the power to bless you beyond measure. Satan tries so hard to deceive us into thinking that if we leave the choice with God, He'll take advantage of us and we will miss out on the best. Satan gets us to believe that God has this homely lady with long, curly hair – and that's just below the knees! – that He's been trying to find a husband for, and now that you've said you will marry whoever He picks, He finally has found someone to dump her off on. Is this reality? No way!

God has lavished upon us gifts far greater than we deserve, giving us His only Son and eternal life with Him. As Hudson Taylor said, God does "give the very best to those who leave the choice to Him."

As a single person, I knew that God wouldn't let me down. I asked myself once, "Will I ever wish I hadn't trusted God so much?"

I answered immediately, "No! I'll only wish I had trusted Him more."

When I gaze into the eyes of my beautiful wife over the delicious, candle-lit dinner she's prepared, and I am overwhelmed with love for her, I echo those words again: I only wish I had trusted Him more. He knew what was best all along.

God created romance to be lifelong and exclusive, because it's a picture of how He loves us. He never splits up with us, He will never dump us, and He wants us to love Him above all else. He wants to be our all-in-all.

I want to close this chapter with a poem that I often read while I was single and struggling with infatuation. This really captures the heart of what we have been trying to say in this book.

SATISFIED

Everyone longs to give themselves completely to someone;
To have a deep soul relationship with another – to be loved thoroughly
and exclusively.
But God says to the Christian:

"No, not until you are satisfied, fulfilled, and content with being loved by
Me alone;
With giving yourself totally and unreservedly to Me;
With having an intensely personal and deep relationship with Me alone.
Discovering that only in Me is your satisfaction found
Will you be capable of the perfect human relationship that I have planned
for you.
You will never be united to another until you are united with Me
Exclusive of any other desire or longing.
I want you to stop planning, stop wishing,
And allow Me to give you the most thrilling plan existing –
And that you can imagine.
I want you to have the best.
Please allow Me to bring it to you
You just keep watching Me, expecting the greatest things,
Keep experiencing the satisfaction that I am,
Keep listening and learning the things that I tell you.
You just wait – that's all
Don't be anxious, don't worry
Don't look at the things others have gotten –
Or at what I have given them.
You just keep looking up to Me –
Or you will miss what I want to show you.
And then, when you are ready,
I'll surprise you with a love far more wonderful
Than any you could dream of.
You see, until you are ready,
And the one I have for you is ready,
(I am working even at this moment to have both of you
Ready at the same time)
Until you are both satisfied exclusively with Me
And the life I have prepared for you,
You won't be able to experience the love
That exemplifies your relationship with Me
And this is the perfect love.
Dear one, I want you to have this most wonderful love;
I want you to see in the flesh a picture of your relationship with Me,
And to enjoy materially and concretely the everlasting union
Of beauty, perfection and love I offer you with Myself.
Know that I love you utterly, for I am God.
Believe it, and be satisfied."

CHAPTER 14

HOPE FOR THOSE WHO HAVE MESSED UP

I have spoken quite strongly about the consequences of immorality, and I'm sure there are many of you who have read all this and were filled with remorse and shame, or perhaps you felt condemned. I'm sorry if that is how I came across. I have a small son, and when he gets close to the oven, I speak sharply to him because I want to spare him the pain and consequences of a burn. But if he ever gets burned, I have no desire to condemn him for making a wrong choice. The pain in his hand is consequence enough. If you have been burned by violating God's design, I don't want to make the pain worse. My desire is to call you to the One who can bring healing. No matter how many times you have messed up, it is never too late to bring your love life to God, and put Him back in charge. Sin has consequences, but God can bring healing and protect you from more pain. In this chapter, I want to share the hope and forgiveness of Christ to all those who are feeling broken and in need of repair.

I know God has forgiven me, but I still feel so much guilt about my past. How can I learn to forgive myself?

Satan is a master liar and when we are under his attack it is so easy to justify our actions. It's ironic that while he tempts us, the enemy tells us that this sin is no big deal. Then afterward, he changes his tune and torments us with how terrible we were to commit that sin! He loves to drag us down with guilt. He knows that when we feel under a cloud of guilt, our communion with God is broken. God feels distant and aloof.

Our feelings of guilt are real and an indication of the wrong we have done and the condemnation we deserve. But Jesus gave His life for us, taking that condemnation on Himself. Paul tells us that there is now no condemnation to those who are in Christ Jesus (Romans 8:1). God's purpose for guilt is that it drives us to Him, not drives us away! Guilt can show us how much we need our Savior's empowerment and forgiveness. Jesus gave everything He had so that we could be free from this burden of guilt and enter God's presence boldly and joyfully. He wants you to be in rich, life-giving fellowship with Him. He wants you to feel the exhilaration of being pure and holy!

I have struggled with feelings of guilt and self-condemnation, but

God showed me that His assessment of the situation was much more important than mine. When I chose to stay mired in my guilt, I was denying my Savior the fruit of His Cross. It is such a shame to stay stuck in mud and slavery when Jesus paid an unfathomable price for us to be clean and free!

Ultimately, being freed from guilt is not simply forgiving yourself, but learning to see your life accurately from God's perspective. God doesn't just want you to feel good, He wants to take your life and actually free you from the bondage of sin. He wants to heal the damage that your wrong choices and the wrong choices of others have caused in your life. He wants His Spirit indwelling you; the communion you'll feel with His Holy Spirit will cover over the feelings of guilt and condemnation.

Let your guilt drive you into the loving and comforting arms of your Savior.

Below I have personalized some Scriptures that really helped me during my times of guilt. Meditate on these words of your Creator and Savior as His message to you. Let His Word change your perspective and rest in His overwhelming love!

> Dearest Child,
>
> I want you to know how much I truly love you. Yes, I've loved you with an everlasting love; with loving kindness I have drawn you to Me. I have searched you and known you. I know about your sitting down and your rising up; I understand your thoughts from afar. I comprehend your path, and am acquainted with all your ways. I have hedged you behind and before; I have laid My hand on you. I know that such knowledge is too wonderful for you. It is so high you cannot attain it.
>
> But where can you go from My Spirit, or where can you flee from My presence? If you ascend into heaven, I am there. If you make your bed in the depths, I am there as well. If you take the wings of the morning, or dwell in the uttermost parts of the sea, even there My hand shall lead you, and My right hand shall hold you. The darkness shall not hide you; the darkness and the light are both alike to Me.
>
> I created every part of you. I tenderly covered you in your mother's womb. You were not hidden from Me while I skillfully knit your skeleton. I saw you even before you were formed.
>
> You are truly precious in My sight – how often I think of you! If you could count the times, they would number more than the sands of the sea. The thoughts I have of you are plans of

peace and not of evil, to give you a future with hope!

Fear not, I am with you. Don't be dismayed, for I am your God. I will strengthen you, yes, I will help you. I hold you in My hand.

All the days I have fashioned for you are written in My book. I set the number of days you have on this earth before you even existed, and nothing can shorten them. You are Mine, little one, and no one can snatch you from My hands. Oh how I love you! Abide in My love. I will quiet you with My love, and rejoice over you with singing.

Precious child, do not despise My chastening, for whom I love, I chasten. I do this for your profit, that you may partake of My holiness. Behold, eye has not seen, nor ear heard, nor has it even entered into the heart of man the things that I have prepared for those who love Me.

You love Me, because I first love you. You know, there is no greater love than to lay down one's life for his friend. This is even how you know love, because I laid down My life for you.

Oh, that you could comprehend the width and length and depth and height of My love which surpasses knowledge. For what shall separate you from My love? Shall tribulation, or distress, or persecution, or famine, or peril, or sword? There is nothing, not death nor life, nor angels nor principalities nor powers, nor things present nor things to come, nor any other created thing, that shall ever be able to separate you from My love.

Child, not even your sins can separate you from my love. I wish you could see the depth of my grace! Reason with me: Though your sins are as scarlet, I can make you so that you are as white as snow. Forget the former things; do not dwell on the past! I, even I, am He who blots out your transgressions, for My own sake, and remembers your sins no more!

Think about these things, my dear child... if I am for you, who can be against you? Who can bring a charge against you? I am the One who justifies you! Who is the one condemning you? I died in your stead, rose from the dead, and I am at the right hand of my Father, pleading for you! Who does that leave? Who is making you feel guilty?

Do you have any idea how much I paid so that you could walk away from your sins and be free from them? Why do you ignore My finished work! I said, "It is finished!" There is nothing more you can do to atone for your sin. If you will agree with me and admit that what you did was wrong, I promise you I will forgive your sins and cleanse you from all unrighteousness. Child, listen to me: Your sins are forgiven for My name's sake! Your sins are forgiven, so go and sin no more. Even if your heart condemns you, I am greater than your heart, and know all things.

If I set you free, you will be free indeed. It is for freedom that I have set you free. Stand firm then! Don't let yourself be burdened again by a yoke of slavery. My mercies are new every morning. Accept what I have done. Nothing you have done can justify you in My sight. I became sin for you. I give you My righteousness. When My Father looks at you, He doesn't see your sins. They were all wiped away at the cross for those who put their faith in Me. You stand clean before Me. Because of the cross, you are blameless. Believe Me when I tell you your sins are forgiven you. Go and sin no more! Without Me, you can do nothing. But through Me, you can do whatever I ask of you!

I love you dearly!!

Your God and Savior,

Jesus Christ

Scripture references used in this letter: Jer. 31:3, Ps. 139, Is. 43:4, Jer. 29:11, Is. 41:10, John 10:28, John 15:9, Zeph. 3:17, Heb. 4:5-6,10, 1 Cor. 2:9, 1 John 4:19, John 15:13, 1 John 3:16, Eph. 3:18-19, Rom. 8:35,38-39, Is. 1:18; 43:18,25, Rom. 8:31-34, John 19:13, 1 John 1:9; 2:12, John 8:11, 1 John 3:20, John 8:36, Gal. 5:1, Rom. 3:20, 2 Cor. 5:21, John 15:1, Phil. 4:13.

PURITY COMMITMENT

I acknowledge that love, sex, and romance are gifts from God to be enjoyed solely in the context of lifelong commitment. God has given us guidelines for these gifts because he knows the terrible consequences that inevitably follow when these gifts are misused.

I choose to submit my life and desires to the lordship of the One who died to make me whole. I choose to begin loving my future spouse today by committing to begin praying for my future spouse. I make a covenant before God not to look lustfully at someone I am not married to. I will seek to avoid defrauding a member of the opposite gender, either by touch, words, or immodest dressing, in any way that would stir up desires that I cannot righteously fulfill. I will instead seek to love the members of the opposite gender the way Christ would with purity and a servant's heart.

I acknowledge that only God can fulfill my deepest longings and that until I am satisfied by Him alone, I am not ready to love a spouse the way that God intends.

I acknowledge that I belong to my Creator. During these single years I will pour my energies into knowing God and developing my gifts and talents for His glory. I know that I will fail and make mistakes, but I pledge to repent of my wrongdoing and accept the forgiveness that was purchased by my Savior on the cross. I repent of my past immoral actions and look to my Savior to bring restoration and wholeness where there was pain and brokenness.

God is the inventor of pleasure. He gave me my desires for love and sexual fulfillment; He is the only one who knows how to truly satisfy these desires. I trust Him to bring fulfillment in His time and in His way.

_____   _____

Name   Date

END NOTES

Introduction

p. 7 Divorce statistics – www.divorcemag.com

Chapter 4

p. 53 J. Budziszewski, "Outside of marriage there's not a chance for that kind of intimacy..." How to Stay Christian in College, p 88-89, (Colorado Springs: NavPress, 1999)

Chapter 9

p. 95 "the story of columnist Mark Trahant..." Les and Leslie Parrot, Love Talk, p 37, (Grand Rapids,MI: Zondervan, 2004)

p. 95 "In an era of increasingly fragile marriages,..." B. J. Fowers, "Psychology and the good marriage: Social theory as practice," American Behavioral Scientist 41 (1998): 516-26

p. 107 "Wiio's Laws..." http://www.cs.tut.fi/~jkorpela/wiio.html

Chapter 10

p. 121 C.S. Lewis quote on masturbation – Illustrations for Biblical Preaching, p. 236, (Grand Rapids, Michigan: Baker Book House: fourth printing 1991)

p.122 "According to one study" – Internet Filter Review, www.blazing-grace.org/cms/bg/pornstats

p. 125 "In a ChristiaNet.com poll" - http://christiannews.christianet.com/1187623495.htm

Chapter 11

p. 131 C. S. Lewis, "Pride leads to every other vice: it is the great anti-God state of mind." Mere Christianity, p. 110, (New York: Touchstone, 1996.)

p. 133 G. K. Chesterton "Alice must grow small if she is to be Alice in Wonderland." Heretics/Orthodoxy, p. 248-249, (Nashville:Thomas Nelson, 2000.)

Chapter 12

p. 147 "It was a song about the little footprints" – "Little Footprints", Steve Fox, Lunch with Chet (2007)

p. 149 Satisfied poem – author unknown

CONTACT INFORMATION

If you have any questions or comments or would like to order additional copies of the book, contact the author:

Jesse and Heidi Jost
PO Box 314
Milk River, Alberta T0K1M0
Canada

Phone: 1(403) 647-2438

Email: jhjost@gmail.com

Or you can order online:

www.purityandtruth.com

www.josephinepublishing.com

www.josties.com

www.heartsathome.ca
(click on Store tab)